Barney White Rats

Jack May

John the Baptist

Swagger Country

Also by Jim Henderson

War:

GUNNER INGLORIOUS
R.M.T.
22 BATTALION
UNOFFICIAL HISTORY

Peace:

TOBACCO FARM
TE KAO 75
ONE FOOT AT THE POLE
NEW ZEALAND'S SOUTH ISLAND IN COLOUR
OPEN COUNTRY
RETURN TO OPEN COUNTRY
OPEN COUNTRY CALLING
OUR OPEN COUNTRY
OPEN COUNTRY MUSTER
THE NEW ZEALANDERS (with James Siers)

Swagger Country

Jim Henderson

line drawings by
MARK DUNSTAN

HODDER AND STOUGHTON
AUCKLAND   LONDON   SYDNEY

Copyright © 1976 by Jim Henderson.
First Printed 1976.
ISBN 0 340 209275
All rights reserved.

No part of this publication may be reproduced or transmitted in any form or by any means electronic or mechanical, including photocopy, recording or any information storage retrieval system without permission in writing from the publisher.

Printed and bound in New Zealand for Hodder and Stoughton Ltd., 52 Cook Street, Auckland, by Wright and Carman Ltd., Trentham.

CONTENTS

Chapter		Page
1	What Price Threepence?	1
2	On the Trail of John the Baptist	7
3	Ray Kirk's 'Who's Who' of Canterbury Swaggers	26
4	Violet Kerr Meets 'The Shiner'. An Immortal Swagger	42
5	Two Shiners	50
6	'The Fattening Paddock'	64
7	Grandmother's Extraordinary Confinement	80
8	Jack May Swags Today	88
9	'You've Got To Pocket Your Pride'	95
10	Russian Jack Vos Beautiful!	100
11	'Man Oh Man, I Vos Free!'	105
12	Women Concerned	114
13	'Anyhow Jesus Wandered Around'	131
14	'The Starlight Boarding House Fraternity'	147
15	Dags	160
16	'She Could Have Nearly Howled	172

What Price Threepence?

The wineberry tree grew out from the edge of the house by the back door—you won't see it there now, the whole lot went up in flames, burned down to ashes years ago—and right alongside was a great trunk of wood like a butcher's block with the separator fixed on top, and a shaft coming out of the separator works had a small split in it; a great place to cram in a wineberry leaf and then turn the handle and send the leaf roaring round.

    The wineberry tree had a smooth just-right kind of trunk for a small hand, just the place to lean one hand and arm against while turning the separator properly—I mean no leaf or twig fooling around this time—the skim milk pouring out of the bottom spout goodoh and creek-edge frothing into the dirty old dented calf bucket in its glory once a shining Gold Plume petrol tin before the farmer or Darcy or the gangling stumbling slipping worker dad called 'Quangle-Wangle' (surely his bootlaces couldn't have been coming undone ALL the time?) cut the top out, banged the rough sharp bits down flat with a noisy echoing hammer, knocked in a couple of holes to thread across a Number 8 wire handle, and there was a milking bucket! just like that, to serve its time under the cracked and carrot-like teats of Old Bluey, until it grew old and grey and was humbled into a smelly and carelessly washed who-cares calf bucket.

 The cream came out of the top spout of the separator in a thin trickle. All hell broke loose, leaking like the *Lusitania,* if you DIDN'T keep turning that handle, you know. The cream trickled slowly into a white enamel pie dish. Sometimes a glass bowl they made red jelly in, or custard, or the lovely Queen Pudding, or heaped with raspberries in January. The bottom took ages to cover. Mittens the black cat with a white daisy on his chest wasn't the only one at times watching with envy (face a bit like a morepork now and then, come to think of it: would the mice agree?) that cream circling and spreading slowly . . . cream sopping right through fresh bread sliced hot and floury from the oven tins now with rich red glossy raspberry jam sloshed thick over it—aha!—or making dreamy satisfying riverbed patterns in the second helping of plentifully sugared stewed red plums picked from that big tree down the bottom of the orchard . . .

 Round the corner came the swagger, more a bent shadow than anything else in the dusk except his boots scraped once with a humble throat-clearing sound as he crossed over the concrete path to the clothes line, past the separator, and knocked at the back door.

 One-two-three.
 What an enormous swag on his back. In the dusk.
 Not Father Christmassy at all.
 Hunchback . . .? Hunchback of Notre Dame . . .?
 He leaned, lifted one foot, slowly put it down, lifted the other, as if they were hot.

What Price Threepence?

Mum came to the back door, wiping her hands on her sugarbag apron, the light strong behind her, smells from the kitchen too, I guess, and a thought there may have been leeks and white sauce to go with the roast mutton and roast potatoes and parsnips and gravy, chuckling rich brown steaming gravy lapping the lot, and . . .

Well, I do hope he was invited into the kitchen for a thorough good feed and a really good warm. This would have been winter or late autumn, and high up on the hill, and frost starts forming in the shadows by some of those road bends before the sun goes down, and I could take you to some places, not counting the gravel pit and things like that, where the frost on the grass blades and bits of clay and fern doesn't go away all day.

If he went into the kitchen or not, carefully wiping his boots first you can be sure, I don't know. I THINK his swag came off, with a bit of a thump, to rest for a while on the back step, the black cat stalking off stiff and haughty and social conscious, putting on an act as cats and people do, but I couldn't swear to it.

I DO remember him though standing in the dark by the back door (near the separator, the demoted calf tin) and stowing away newspaper-wrapped packets in his pockets or perhaps in some small bag or pouch within his old tweedy coat—his swag was up on his shoulders anyhow, lumpy, hunchbacked, like something crouching there for protection against the frosty stars and the wolverine profiles of the shelterbelt pinetrees—and a warm voice saying, mum's undoubtedly: "There's bread. And that's a bit of butter to go with it. Some cheese, just a bit, not worth mentioning, we're not cheesy people. There's those few hunks of cold meat, yes, with a couple of chops. That's it. Now take the tea, screwed up in this, don't let it get too loose, and . . . yes . . . there's some sugar in with it, not much, but a bit. There you are now."

And there, clearest of all, forever, rummaging, rummaging, rummaging somewhere (how EXACTLY that word has it, there in the doorstep dark and the cold) and saying: "I can pay for it. Oh I can pay for it": and then holding out the palm of his right hand, there may have been more than one coin on it, but certainly to lighthouse across Time there right in the middle of the hand shone the small threepenny bit, of course refused, and away he went, to camp in a derelict hut a few miles on up the main road near Jack Drummond's place just opposite that turnoff leading out over the rocks and through the stumps to Canaan (oh God, why Canaan, wasn't it bitter enough as it was?) and a policeman came winding and steering (handcuffs in HIS pockets?) all the way up from Motueka a day or two later to arrest him as a vagrant someone reckoned when they thought I wasn't listening, and for nights after, for many many nights after, sunk deep in bed with the light out and the wind stalking the shelterbelt, the wineberry watching, I'd be crying silently, nobody heard, seeing that swagger's hand and the proffered shining silvery threepence.

Mr Palmer was quite different. I know nothing about his coming, his going, how long he stayed—briefly, and without much comfort I fear, not much human acknowledgment, while within we listened wide-eyed to heroics about another swagger who also felt the going long and the wind cold: nightly helpings of Walter Scott's *The Lay of the Last Minstrel*, the beautiful young schoolteacher fairhaired from Wakefield who stayed with us teaching her first five pupils, nodding approval . . .

How typical that seems of those days, the 1920s when our hearts were supposed to beat 12,000 miles away, in a country called 'Home' we had never seen . . . bracken, not fern . . . nightingales, not tuis . . . rills and brooks not creeks, bluebells in the woods, never clematis the faithful bride of every spring even bandaging the stumps of the slain and burnt bush in the new clearings out the back . . .

Suddenly, like a Jack in the Box, another swagger, Mr Palmer was there, briefly at work, scything in style in the sun and in a contemplative manner, the long grass on a small slope between the front of the house and the shrubbery, young shining leafed rata marking the boundary of his scything on the right, some miserable hydrangea cuttings defining the left perimeter, and in the middle a hopeful young scarlet oak, its trunk as thick as a wooden jamspoon.

Mr Palmer must have been very old, all that white hair, yet he had a baby face and the softest voice I had ever heard.

His words went on, they seemed to ripple, they seemed to be friends of his, he enjoyed them. Even the way the sun shone through his hair was part of the gentleman about him—I could never see Mr Palmer wrenching up the slimy nose of a sheep in the yards to see if it was a two-tooth.

As he swished and sliced and the dandelions and another white-headed thing fell terribly before him, Mr Palmer spoke of the French Revolution. Spoke appreciatively, and underlined parts, by pausing to whet, with a tremendous rasping noise like a dozen gullets going west, his great long fearsome blade with a sharpening stone resembling a small vengeful handy white bone.

"There were all those aristocrats"—Swish—"and all those rich people"—Swish—"with all their wonderful clothes and carriages"—Swish—"and servants. Feasts and banquets! And candlelight!" Mr Palmer is saying again over the years. "And important people and people making speeches and knowing every blessed thing about everything.

"People bowing down to them. And stepping out of the way when their carriages went past. Getting splashed by the mud as their carriages went past.

"Then suddenly"—Mr Palmer is severing a clump of red clover, much to the annoyance of a labouring draught-horse of a bumble bee—"Revolution!

"They never knew until it was upon them. Heaped upon them. They were the last to know. Extraordinary! Into the carts, not carriages now, no!—common old carts now like loads of turnips,"—another surprised semi-circle of heads severed with their stalks—"along the streets *with the mud coming back at them now!* . . . to the guillotine . . . then, SNICK! . . . off with their heads!"

Mr Palmer near the end of the slope now, where it's steepest. End of the slope very close.

The back of his knees gave him away, even within those worn grey trousers with a strap round one ankle, his idea of a bowyang perhaps, doing his best. The back of his knees would suddenly bend—just a little too much where the slope became steeper. He'd catch his balance just in time, and look surprised. "Useless old fool," I remember a man's voice saying, not dad's, certainly not. "Quite useless. Always in the way. Give him his swag and get him on the road again."

Angry tongues of fire from the house lashed and licked away half the rata bush, blistered from top to bottom and practically killed the scarlet oak. It's almost dark now, within the ten-foot high thicket of hydrangeas which have outgrown, bled away, all their colour into the slope. They have taken over the slope now where once Mr Palmer stood like Father Time, scything, and telling me about the French Revolution.

Nobody ever harnessed up old Dick the dozey white and often muddy horse to take the old man and his swag to the main road with a couple of bob for the service car—never even harnessed up the sledge—or, growing sinister now in the shadows in the shed, a cart!

On The Trail of John the Baptist

CREMATION SOCIETY OF CANTERBURY
Canterbury Crematorium

Memorial

Robert Ellie Known as John the Baptist Aged 72 Died 9th May 1947
BLOCK. D.F

"Who were they, these swaggers, eh Ray?"
"Just human beings. A life span away. That's all."
"Yes. That'ud be right . . ."
"But that's not enough!" cried Ray Kirk, sitting up exactly

like Jackie, steering his bleached blue Morris Minor 1952, 140,000 miles on the clock, rattly gearbox, noisy tappets, good tyres, Warrant of Fitness. It went. The diffy moaned and groaned. Steering his swagger-of-a-car with aplomb and ceremony through the smog and the smug suburbs of Christchurch.

We were off to see the grave of John the Baptist, the place where they put his ashes away into the earth. The end of that long, long road for this famed swagger, with a permanent address at last, among standard roses.

"Try to put yourself in their place, if you can—you can't really though unless you've been a swagger yourself, I suppose.

"But get a gink of this.

"Think of them sleeping under a hedge, and—boy!—next morning waking with everything white stiff with frost. Maybe some mornings they didn't WANT to wake up. Can't blame 'em."

Ray threaded between two cyclists, turned a corner, and lit a smoke, all simultaneously it seemed to me sitting beside him.

"Man's inhumanity to man . . . Hmmm . . . That accounts for a good deal of it, wouldn't you say? We're a cruel lot, can be. Hmmm . . .

"A Canterbury frost—worse still an Otago frost, and they can be pretty grim up Wanganui way too when they want to, come to think of it. Looked out the pub window once early one morning either at Otaki or Levin. Always mix those two up. Looked out from upstairs and the frost was GRIM!

"Imagine out in that, a night out. Unfolding yourself like a carpenter's rule. Gee! No wonder they took to the meths."

"Cheer up Ray, we're on our way to the Crematorium."

"Ha!"

Ray Kirk, retired at last to his cottage in Dover Street. Worked for the Christchurch City Council in the Depression, "when I wore the Sugar Bag as a relief worker, on the number 5 Scheme"; the Gas Company, "you sure get around a city with a gas company"; the Ministry of Works; then Hygieologist for the Internal Affairs, before retiring.

Howzat again?

Hygieologist, yes, that's right. Top brass passing Ray having a spell and a smoke in his cubbyhole, door partly ajar, spots 'Hygieologist' on door, asks mystified: "What the hell does he do here?" "B . . . . if I know," replies other bit of brass, then hopefully: "Could belong to the Medical Section?"

A lifetime labouring, fixing, mending, wheelbarrowing, digging, swinging the old banjo, the bucket, the broom. He'd spent so much of his time toiling in the open, the wind and the rain, he had a natural sympathy for swaggers.

"Any relation to Norm Kirk by any chance, Ray?"

"Leave that to them to find out."

(Ray didn't go politicians of any breed much.)

He himself was a natural historian as well, a lover of everyday things, with an awareness they could pass and blow away leaving no mark or sign and nobody would ever know . . .

More than anyone else Ray was sweeping up swaggers for me like a housewife sweeping up crumbs—Happy Harry, Shiny Bob, an old Syrian woman swagger, a Chinese swagger "who made vegetables under the moon the kids reckoned", Hayseed, Barney the Bull, Goldtooth, Fishy, Gentleman Jim; but these, and more, are to make their appearance over the hill and onto these pages later—because he, too, simply felt for the sake of what our mountain and foothill and plain, concrete culvert dripping and raw clay cutting (with the hen-beak pick marks of the old roadman and roadmakers still there years later, like Babylon's writing-bricks, if you looked carefully and reverently), for what these and the wayside scrub and the lonesome pine, scraggy as an old hen's backside in autumn, and the sighing shelter-belt had seen, the old swaggers *should not be forgotten.*

"Where do you lie, John the Baptist? Who were you? Where did you come from?"—these questions began haunting Ray as his interest fed on his frustrations. Someone told him among other suggestions that he thought the old swagger could have had a short name like Eli—John Eli, or Ely; E. Lay or Lee; or even Cecil A. Early? Buried Bromley cemetery? Died 1954, or 1940? Pauper's grave . . . no, nothing there. Died, killed, or injured in High Street . . . no Brougham Street . . . no Byron Street . . . So few, and such conflicting, reports! After sparetime detective work inquiring over three months— library, police, newspaper, undertaker, certain old Sydnenham barmen—he triumphantly came up with the old swagger's surname, purely by accident.

Out in the car he heard his wife, casually talking about some girl, say "Ellie". Excited, elated, he pulled the car to the side of the road and stopped.

"How would you spell 'Ellie'?"

"E-l-l-i-e, of course."

Ellie it was, the penny had dropped indeed, and soon he tracked him down to the crematorium.

Ray said a car had got John the Baptist in his old age, walking stick and all, cleaned him up in Byron Street close to home when he'd packed in his swaggering days. Stinking cars. This way they'd brought him, dabbed with a discreet disinfectant, neatly tidied up and beard trimmed, that beard he'd started growing back in the '30s when somebody swiped his razor when he was camping out one night by the roadside . . .

His chips handed in, his swag long unrolled and dispersed . . . .

"Ah! Back in the '30s you'd see Johnnie passing through Hornby playing away on his mouth organ and a little yodelling along the south road, the kids following behind him like the Pied Piper of Hamelin," Ray went on fondly.

(Verily, verily a Walt Disney scene in all its nougatness, far from typical as far as tramps and kids are concerned. In reality, most of them would reach for a stone, or a cutting playground chant, as many a bewhiskered old reader will guiltily agree.)

"Yodelling and song and his mouth organ . . .

"He'd entertain the shearers on the station in the season, playing and yodelling for hours, why up to two in the morning sometimes. It was a change to hear John instead of the sheep."

"I'll go for that, Ray! What was he like?"

"Well I saw him mostly coming into town. He'd turn up round town at different times, staying around the city more in his later years.

"Well he was a slender little bloke I'd say. A longish beard, greying going white. A twinkle in his eye, too right, ready at any moment to break out, start to yodel, shift his feet—you know, doing the light fantastic and finishing off, rounding off with a tune on the mouth organ at the finish.

"Ah, you'd see him coming into the pub, the New City, his stick over one arm, the other holding a cabbage or a cauli or something like that. Sometimes a bunch of carrots, ha! the tops sticking out of his overcoat pocket . . . Oh John, good God . . . So the boys would sing out:

" 'What you got today, John?'

"So-an-so, he'd tell them, a bit of tucker, a couple of bob maybe.

" 'Right; give you a bit more for the song and dance act.'

"Into action he'd go."

"Nice, nice, Ray."

Ray said he was a familiar sight all right, this colourful character, frequenting the hotels and doing all right for himself, never fear. What a pity this—yes—you could say lovable oldtimer, met his untimely death the way it happened. "Today forgotten. Tomorrow reborn in talks and stories in years to come."

Sometime around late April or May, you'd see him come homing back to Christchurch for the winters between 1935 and 1940, getting under cover somewhere, or taking refuge in the Salvation Army's old man's home in Christchurch. "Springtime he was away, back to his haunts of days gone by, roaming round."

Age increasing. His Sydenham friends started to look after him a bit. "Sydenham," as Ray described it, "gnawed away with the borer and the bulldozer."

SC 2

You'd see him playing outside a factory in St Asaph Street, where a bob was to be made—he knew where—such as the Bus Depot, his keen eyes picking out a mate or an old acquaintance of days gone by. Naturally, knowing John was not there to inquire about his health, the traveller would feel in his back pocket, hand over a coin or two: "On your way, John", and with a yodel he'd be off. Dressed in his overcoat in Cathedral Square, placing his old felt hat on the footpath in front of his boots, then letting rip with his mouth organ.

"John was a loner in the town, you never saw him with a mate."

And so to the last call in Byron Street, a hellava dusty murky place there close to the railway lines (smoke, coal) and the big gasworks full of smoke, as Ray described it.

John the Baptist had a room at Sidney Roy Tolchard's two-storey place, 45 Byron Street, facing south, loved by the all-day lingering frosts, the quaint old cottages of those days now mercifully rooted away into rubbish by the wild boar bulldozers; demolished for factories, workshops.

The house, explained Ray, would get little more than a couple of hours sun in the winter; damp, an iceberg, nicely perfumed by the smoke from the railway yards in the murky winter months, the east winds bringing the odours from the gasworks. Can *anyone* wonder why the country roads and the lights and the yap and swill of the boozers called. Even sleeping under a bridge—arrrr hell . . .

"The northerly view was magnificent: goods sheds and the backsides of buildings on Carlyle Street."

The rooms of these houses were match-lined and papered, typical family homes of the early 1900s. Sydenham in its heyday was the cheapest part to live, in 'our most English city', 'the Cathedral city'. Carlyled and Byroned.

"Chuff-shuff of the engine wheels skidding on icy rails in the shunting yards—the rattle of trucks heard for miles on a still night—shrieking echoing whistles of the engine—how the hell the residents slept I don't know."

The time on Friday night was between 9.00 and 9.15 p.m.

A dark place where he was hit, in Byron Street. Picked up by St John Ambulance driver, William Robert ("Doughy") Palmer, died in the Public Hospital from severe head and other injuries, then collected for last attentions from Albert Henry Marker, of Lamb and Haywards, undertakers, at 292 Cashel Street.

"We had a heavy fog on the Sunday, 11th of May, after John's death."

On Saturday morning, Harry Gunn—he kept a greengrocery shop opposite the Provincial Hotel in Cashel Street and served there as a part-time barman—began a collection for a few wreaths for the old chap he'd known for years. The tarpaulin muster collected £31.6.6., which was made to cover all charges including a Public Thanks notice in the two newspapers, the barmen doing their share in passing the hat round.

"Don't worry about payment," Albert the undertaker told the concerned Harry, who incidentally had been a wellknown New Zealand boxer. "More important is to fix John's funeral."

Albert arranged with the Rev. Winton, a Presbyterian minister of St Peters Presbyterian Church in Ferry Road, to take the service at the crematorium chapel in Linwood Avenue at 4.15 p.m. on Monday. He also fixed, on behalf of his firm, a memorial rose tree and a plaque for the old swagger.

The police couldn't find any relatives, but they said he'd been born at Clapham, London, in 1880, (yet 'Aged 72, died 1947', says the crematorium card). Year of arrival in New Zealand 1926. Original occupation, seaman. Single. But his death certificate says 67, London born, labourer, 26 years in New Zealand.

'DIED PENNILESS BUT WAS NOT FRIENDLESS', said the newspaper, giving him 7¼ inches.

Harry Gunn said John first had been in Threadneedle Street, working for the Stock Exchange, presumably as a messenger, then away as a sailor to Vancouver, Cape Town, Sydney, coming ashore in New Zealand with a hundred pounds to take to the roads, finally settling on Canterbury and the West Coast.

"He made his last long trip three or four years ago," Harry told that reporter. "Christchurch to Timaru, he reckoned he'd do, and back, but ah, his leg gave out, and he had to give up at Ashburton on the way down. A farmer picked him up and brought him back to Christchurch."

They gave him number 2509 in the crematorium book. About half a dozen mourners came, including Harry Gunn, Albert Marker, Goldie Stack, Tom Gill.

The crematorium chimney, much taller than all those thousands of telegraph poles passed and marking off his time by the roads, sent a faint smoke and haze into the sky as we got out of the car.

"Hmm. Block DF. Now where's that?"

Hunting until we found his small soft weatherbeaten stone about half the size of a milepeg among all the rosebushes and the neatly dividing little paths too small for any car to swoop and slay. There, between Matilda Read 17.3.49 (left), and Peter and Jessie McDougall, 48 and 72, (right):

ROBERT ELLIE
Known as
John the Baptist
9.5.47

The standard rose—sturdy secure suburban—alongside his stone wasn't in flower. "A Madam DuPont. Tended for many years by Scotty Campbell," said Ray. Should we have brought him something? A warming drop of whisky? I'd thought, but only thought, before we'd got into the car, of taking a handful of rose petals for the old chap, or would dog daisies from a clay cutting or buttercups with more-than-gold-gloss be more apt?

Echoes would begin (and the thought of a childhood ear pressed against a late-afternoon telegraph pole "to hear the messages"), vibrations seeking shreds about swaggers from unknown minds around our country, and in they'd come all right, in slow furrow-treading faith, once you had the focal point of a grave, a printed page in a magazine or book.

On the Trail of John the Baptist 15

John the Baptist threading round Christchurch in the 1930's, playing a mouth organ, drunk or sober, happy or hangovered, quaint or a blasted nuisance, then he'd be off. Off past those thousands of acres with thousands of sheep in Canterbury and Marlborough: surely those big cockies would be big of heart, never to grudge a passing crumb? Not necessarily so! The "Hungry M . . .s" with their meanness so exasperated a housemaid that, vowing to give 'em economy, she henceforth flung dead mice from the traps into the ever-bubbling stock pot which everybody in the kitchen from then on took good care never to sample.

The station, said Annie Kirk, where the shearers asked for mustard. "Mustard? Mustard?" shouted the wife, as if little Oliver Twist himself stood humbly before her. "What do they want mustard for with their mutton? Oh the huge brutes!"

Off up the East Coast, swag up, Kaikoura to Kekerengu, sixty miles of take-it-away coast, inland in winter the peaks like blue jelly and whipped cream; ribboning the coast road and swirling the dust Rink Taxis shouting, "We'll have a crack at Newmans!"—the breakers bashing and grinding the gravel, tossing the whalebones, combing the kelp, grieving the old wreck by the mouth of the Clarence River, great rocks sprawled in dejected or prehistoric attitudes half-sunk in despair if you put your mind to it and they become almost unbearable if you peel back a little more of your imagination's layers (just like Kipling's 'Boots—boots—boots—boots—movin' up an' down again')—Ward and Seddon, ('Mr Speaker! I wish to draw the House's attention to . . .' ha ha! dust to you too, old acrobats with our money until we realise with rage, playing the fool with our lives, too, monkey-swinging with our very lives); Altimarloch, a bit off Blenheim's main road, mind you, but the call of the honeysuckle and the wild bees in the rafters, the creek right by the backdoor bricks, the sleek fat turkeys (knock one off with a good hefty swipe with a stick in the night! What a feed! Bits in the bottom of the bag too for days afterwards, lovely! But only in thought—don't queer your pitch, man), perching and peering anxiously ('What was that in the dark?

Oh dear oh dear, whatever possessed the family to migrate to this lost land in the first place?') from their guanoed teetering roosts on the shells of old decayed willow trees never to be forgotten, that's Marlborough too, castled and walled watercourses dry as a brown birch chip with old Matagouri mumbling in his mad thorns; dusty, bronzed, with a whiff of grease from the fleece and longfaced blackandwhite sheepdog laconic in the tussock; Pelorus (the wooden bridge all rock below, hell for the hip, not too good to sleep there if you're shickered or if you don't know your way about), and Rai Valley and the old women making patchwork quilts in the sun; shuffling down Gentle Annie the slanting rain a fair cow in your face; Nelson where the hospital sneaks you a bed for the night on the quiet provided things are slow as usual and the big shots aren't about, and pick me a golden apple from a golden apple tree if nobody's looking; Foxhill where the horsecoaches halted, steam rising and sweat and tired jingles and red-rimmed nostrils with a final snort for the heavy day, and the yellowhammers, and the chaff pouring into the box by the mouseshadowed stall, the stacked earth-floor cellar cool under the pub. Oh let me loose! but it's lace up your boots and away up and into and over the Range to Murchison, the deer vanishing in the fern, lucky the Midnight Butcher of Motupiko didn't get you, then the great wandering sluicing companion to accompany with care, the Buller River:

> Buller River silver grin
> Haul the brash prospector in!
> Buller Buller roar him home
> Grind him down to scream and bone!

The Coast, blackberried and boozing and the world's best cream buns.

They were blowing up the Cobden Hill getting rocks for the Greymouth Harbour breakwater, a great day, the charges had gone off, rocks aplenty were strewn about, to the keen interest of a little, rather insignificant man watching proceedings. This little powerhouse of energy had just arrived in the morning with his full kit, roll, billy, all his gear.

"Hullo," said the shotfirer. "Nice day. It's gone off well, eh? And who are you?"

"I'm John the Baptist."

"Well I be darned! Glad to meet you." They yarned for a bit, then: "And where are you intending to sleep tonight, John?"

"Oh I'll find a place all right. I can look after myself."

"Look: you can doss in the shed if you like."

John did. Later on in the evening the shotfirer, who could have been Paddy Tobin, decided he'd play a joke on John, throwing pebbles on the tin roof. Too true, John was scared, and convinced the hill was about to collapse, took off clutching all his gear under his arms, bounding then staggering on to a good safe distance, where he tidied up his roll before promptly making for Westport the same night.

No wonder after this he favoured the stolid residence of Bottly Lowe, a cavedweller close to the Cobden bridge.

Onward: the higgledy-piggledy mailboxes by the roadside, solitary or in crazy colonies; leaning over a brokenbacked gate and saying to the half-asleep cockie: "Yeah, yeah, that's right, you can bet on it, you must get into it—*next week.*" Then back to Christchurch, getting your back into it by way of Arthurs Pass, standing by the pass, looking down to the plains, catching a sour-sweet whiff of the Provincial round closing time—and the stories, the echoes coming up in the mirage of the years:

'Jack the Mattress', a small child Enid Stone always called him when he came through Windwhistle, mid-Canterbury, where the Stone brothers had a couple of farms, very dusty, whiskery, but not a full beard, around 1929, his possessions wrapped in a dull khaki blanket once obviously a check pattern, and blackened billy on top. "Ye little devils, ye limbs of Satan!" he exclaimed when the youngsters gave corned beef to the dogs. The children remember him reciting a psalm or singing a hymn at the least excuse. A bible in his pack. Give him a wave and he'd always wave back . . .

[Onto the road and away, stride it out for a bit man, suck in the clear air, bite off great sparkling chunks of As-It-Was-In-The-Beginning, away from the frowsy pub, the pub where the merry farmers, between sighs, groans, teethsucking, gazing hopelessly, agonised raking of hobnails for emphasis, hawking like dispirited buzz-saws, and slow heartbroken headshaking, are drinking their subsidies amid a sort of lugubrious ritualistic lowing:
"Things is crook."
"Ahhhhhrrrrr."
"An' they'll get crooker."
"Snow out Deadman's Bush last week. Slips clean through the fences."
"Why don't the Gubbermint do somethink about it eh? I ast yh. Good luck."
"River up real bad."
" 'Put the road through to YOUR place?' says this inspector coot. 'Do yh think we're cuckoo?' "
"Open him up. Took one look. Sewed the poor cow up again. Hopeless."
"Sink blocked for two days now. Tealeaves, the dirty old hooer. Me dog won't come in now."
"Pitiful to see, barleygrass to the horizon. An' more."
"A nail clean through me bastard boot. Compo? Don't make me laugh."
"Been on the toot agen. Break yer heart."
"Deer thick as politicians' nuts. Never seem to go toot though. Nar. Funny, that."
"A tree got him. Lived a week though. In agony."
"Come with his flash new dog. Hooled 'em clean over the bluff. Talk about laugh."
"Caught in the crusher. Both hands."
"Couldn't raise a cupful of super, an' on top of that, the shed goes and blows down."
"The pain all sudden catch me cruel right in the

On the Trail of John the Baptist 19

crutch everybloodytime I bends over to open a gate."
"I think he died in a bushfire."
"Threw her first time. Never the same since."
"A stoat musta got in. All laid out there, me pride an' joy."
"Growth as big as a pumpkin, the quack reckoned."
"Gored by a polled Angus, the fool tried to tell me. God pickle me tit, keep me from townies, the Grey Ones, the Slater People."
"All me swedes gone, clean as a whistle."
"Shift me stock I do. Make no difference. Just look at yh. Keel over dead. Stone dead."
"When it's not rainin' it's blowin'. Hundred Year Flood every autumn takes half me best riverflats."
"Ten years work—an' not worth a cuntful a cold water."
"What's more, 'e cleared off with me Green River, the miserable cow."
"Same agen? Go another drop from Old Darkie—they should a shot him!"
"Fill 'em up. May as well. Old girl's got pulpy kidney by the look uv her."
"Deadly poison turned out to be, see? Lucky to be alive."]

Overhearing another swagger in the pub saying he was off to cook at a station just out of Methven, John craftily finished his beer, sped off, got the job, set up business until next morning, when the dilatory swagger arrived, and was engaged in a furious fight resulting in both being ordered off the station and both departing in different directions exchanging words unsavoury rather than complimentary. As luck would have it, a day later John was in the pub he started out from when in through the doorway came the other fellow. Another donnybrook erupted until this time John discreetly took off for Coalgate.

Before John hit Coalgate or Glentunnel he always washed in the Hororata River or Stream, cleaned himself up, made himself respectable before joining the company of others. He was always raggedy, but clean. Many a time, said Jack

Reynolds of Glentunnel, he'd pick John up on the side of the road sleeping it off, put him in the back of the truck, shove him in the shed for the night under cover. John Ryan saw him once near Dunsandel, heading towards Christchurch, with a set of antlers perched on top of his swag.

Some sourpuss saw John the Baptist removing his pants behind a tree in a park and rang the police—quite unnecessarily, because the swagger apparently at times wore a couple of pairs of pants, the better pair underneath. This time, he was innocently getting down to his better pants, to visit a patient-pal in the public hospital—with a couple of snorts supplied by the Excelsior barman to help him on his way. John favoured taking fish and chips to any pal in hospital.

In a pub in Riccarton some laborious wit doped the old man's beer, cascara or something like that, and poor old John got the skitters suddenly, was forced to drop his tweeds behind a tree, someone saw him, got the cops onto him, and he was lumbered.

Up before the Court once, perhaps because of this embarrassing incident, probably for being disorderly and causing a modest commotion in the Square, he was recognised by one of the detectives who spoke to the magistrate, and John got off with a caution.

He was said to have given the police the lead they sought and needed to capture a fugitive who had committed a murder under provocation in a back country hut.

A policeman "would start him off with a yodel, and John would yodel all the way down Cashel Street."

Good tempered and harmless enough, John the Baptist became annoyed when he thought some people in a tram in Moorhouse Avenue were making fun of him or laughing at him. He broke the window of the tram with his stick, reckons Goldie Stack. He was hustled away from the scene very hastily.

Stewart Watson, who was a boy at Briscoes in Cashel Street, still clearly sees John the Baptist sitting on the low fence of the St Pauls Church, playing his mouth organ. From here, he'd go into Briscoes, opposite the church, and yarn with the blokes, who'd take a collection for him. The cold church wouldn't.

"Don't booze it, John—buy tucker," the Briscoes boys would say.

But these were the years of free counterlunches, so fourpence for a beer then a feed! *He had his entrance money!*

Around the Christmas of 1930, John, mouth organing outside the pubs of Akaroa, was happily earning his beer and tucking zestfully into counterlunches, well-salted thirst encouraging snacks which pubs provided free in those sometimes-good-old-days: cubes of cheese, pickled onions, bits of baked potato piping hot, melted cheese on fingers of toast, pigstrotters, sliced chunks of hot sausages and saveloys, sausage rolls, gherkins, pieces of ham or cold meat, briny olives, fish croquettes, even swiftly-gulped oysters sometimes—not served all at once, of course, but selections from these, generous or mean according to the pub, on plates laid out along the bar counters. During this Akaroa visit, he stayed with Laddy Dierck the Saddler, the steamer *John Anderson*, serving the peninsula, bringing over many an old acquaintance of the road among swaggers, from 50 to 100 of them altogether, drifting in to cut the famous cocksfoot crop without too much effort.

They disembarked at Okains Bay, a stumbling tatterdemalion Legion of the Lost at the world's end. They could go no further.

And they didn't give a damn.

At some stage John had a dog with him. Probably a small black and white one. A pubkeeper put him up for a night. The dog used to sleep in his bed. That was the last time he slept in the pub, the pubkeeper would say with some emphasis.

When someone lonely, wishing for company, offered John the Baptist a home, he replied with a shake of the head: "Goodness me, that would never do. My customers would miss me."

Rounding a bend at Aniseed Point, about ten miles north

of Kaikoura, on St Patrick's Day 1937, Basil Borthwick came upon a party of Kaikoura women enjoying a picnic just as John the Baptist appeared, "swag on back, complete with billy and stick. He was a smallish man, bearded, bright and twinkling eyes, and walking with a springy step.

"Drawing level with the picnic party, he stopped, greetings were exchanged, and he set about entertaining the ladies with some action songs appropriate to St Patrick's Day. They certainly enjoyed his performance and, like Tommy Tucker who sang for his supper, he was invited to share the goodies from the ample picnic baskets."

John once wagered he'd get to Timaru without paying his fare. Watching the guard very carefully, John managed to keep one step ahead of him until the guard began closing in and things were becoming rather tight. John now played his trump card. A woman entered the toilet. As soon as he judged her comfortably seated, he called gruffly: "Guard here. Tickets please. I can't wait. Pass the ticket under the door." John got his ticket all right!

John the Baptist invariably walked in the middle of the road, despite warnings that one day, sure enough, he'd be knocked down . . .

We hang around this tracked-down swagger's full-stop grave for a bit. A wet mist begins to damp my pullover. A week later I'll be hacking and hawking, a soggy sponge laid up in a motel at Haast. Soft. Soft as a puffball, and writing about swaggers . . .

We head back for a feed, then out again, north-west, past the fringe of Christchurch to the Weedons-Ross road, within a mile from the country church on the corner, the way to West Melton.

"That's it. That's where they camped. The Palace."

"We've come just in time Ray. This will have had it soon, too."

"John the Baptist slept here. Ha! Will they ever have a notice up, saying that?"

"For a king of the road!"

"—like Queen Elizabeth? Tim Cane slept in it too."

On the Trail of John the Baptist

Just a grey disintegrating shack, loosening corrugated iron roof, the chimney down and gone, bricks and stones scattered out a few yards into the thirsty close-nibbled paddock beyond the down-at-heel gorse hedge with the remnant of the old gate to block a hole long grown over now. A few dough-faced sheep dopey by the doorway, a propped-up four-bar gate serving as a door, because the door, a faded red, has been slapped on the right-hand wall to fill the gap where the fireplace had been. Jets scratch the sky overhead. The window holes on either side roughly boarded up, yet a flophouse palace this, once upon a time, a comforting shell, a brief warmth, a brief home.

Casual bleached bones at the foot of a half dead tree.

Oh, the long dead-straight roads mile after mile, and the puffy ankles, hot boots, or old boots, or bashed boots, or boots padded with rags or paper and the dust and the inland effortless seagull wheeling momentarily overhead . . . Then the nor'-westers: "Keep yh mouth shut or it'ud blow yh teeth out."

Ray booted a small tin, perhaps a jam tin, eaten with rust, damn near digested:

"The swaggers turning up at the palace—then catching the train into Christchurch—collecting pensions—coming back in the Midland bus to West Melton—getting off—getting boozed—making their way back to the palace, dispersing next day. The months go by. One by one would be absent. Either to the Old Man's Home or had passed on."

Size of hut 26 feet by 18 feet, two main rooms eight by eight and the kitchen at the back extending full length. Initials remain, W.G. and F.T. painted on a wall within. One of the walls had been painted blue!

Mostly stuffed with hay now, the back falling down, a broken-spined effect; sheep and a bird with its nest, the last to camp here inside the back door, both leaving dung behind . . . but there, where the swaggers had stretched and spat and shivered and warmed themselves, where the poorman's altar of the fireplace had been, a bit of ancient linoleum still remains tacked to the wall—This linoleum, faint old green with a casual squiggle couldn't-care-less pattern in it, would have gone round the room in a three-foot tall band originally to make a sort of humble panelling.

Gordon Allison and his friend Bob Wilson at Weedons used to sneak into a similar hut on Wilson's farm when they were kids, Bob told Ray, and get chased out by the swaggers. The adventuring children saw six beds made out of straw with boulders placed around the straw to keep it in place. The beds were in separate rooms neat and tidy, but it's miraculous the whole thing didn't go up in flames a dozen times!

You had to be careful where you walked otherwise you'd go through the floor; the swaggers tended to pull the floorboards up for firing, even rip a bit from off the outside walls, too.

A fight broke out at the hut once, leaving a swagger knocked about and bleeding, lying out in the grassy edge of the road. Along here horses would run, but on this particular day a horse raised suspicions by refusing to go past, and the swagger was found bleeding. The cops questioned the swaggers living there at the time about the affair.

This was a little too much for Tim Cane (Gentleman Jim), one of the brief occupants calling in before resuming their rounds of the countryside. He left, moving on to a hut near Ron Wilson's home—Tim was an honest man. He kept his own time-book, and if he worked seven hours he would put down seven hours. Old man Wilson never queried Tim's time when he worked for a little while on the farm.

"Tim was a cut above the others, and was well up in astrology. They said he was going to be a minister, but turned it in."

Just an old shed now, the palace, with the pleasing slightly dusty smell of hay about, under the loose floorboards merely rusty tins and empty bottles or broken bottles of little interest, not even a painkiller bottle—the collectors must have done it over thoroughly. Not even a decent spiderweb trailing about.

This hut where the swaggers camped is very similar to an

old boot chucked away outside for a couple of years and, alas, about as interesting.

(And after the big storm in August, 1975, Ray would go out for another look at the palace, to find "only the floor remained, covered with rotten straw. Shelley and I just stood there. Me, my mind went back to those days of the past. It was sad you understand", wrote Ray. "I thought of Roger Whittaker singing 'The Last Farewell', picturing him standing there, singing to the remains of the swaggers' hut.")

No ghosts, no echoes, no snatch of ribald song, no reek of powerful socks or whiff of frying eggs "acquired from up by the hedge" to help speculate about this grey Canterbury afternoon.

"Come on. Let's get out of it."

And as we shove off, the old shack rattles like a skeleton in the wind.

And the dense black macrocarpas by Finlay Road.

"Something moved in there."

"Children playing?"

"Ghosties!" says little Shelley.

"The ghost of John the Baptist."

Ray Kirk's 'Who's Who' of Canterbury Swaggers

"I see them now, going up the north road with their smoke-blackened billy, pot, bedroll, and the bowyangs on. One I saw had one gumboot on, his other foot tied up with string and sacking. Imagine the cold Canterbury winters those unfortunates put in, cold, hungry, wet, sick . . .

"What remained for them, when age took its tally? Go on till they dropped? Or finish up at the Old Men's Home in Ashburton, where so many ancient swaggers spent their last days?

"I dare say many of them did the hard yakker, laying the rails of our trunk lines. Old war veterans. In his small way, the swagger certainly was part of the New Zealand life in the early days."

Ray Kirk's 'Who's Who' 27

So wrote Ray Kirk of Christchurch to me, finding more swaggers as his quest for the identity of John the Baptist went on. When Ray finally had tracked down the old swagger among the rosebushes, Ray really had his 'A in G' (backside in gear) as he puts it. His blood now roused, with the dedicated aid and interest of his daughter Myrcine, he went on to round up and record this extraordinary mob of swaggers, almost all of whom soon would have vanished entirely, forgotten, like the mists of the morning over the fields and foothills of Canterbury.

So let's go: we're away.

An old Syrian woman swagger roamed the Waimate area in Canterbury around 1900, a big woman pushing a travel-worn perambulator of pots and pans. The money she earned mending pots and pans fed her. The kids used to cheek her. She would kick her leg out like a mule and tell the kids "to kiss her behind". One or two old chaps of today may have been among those impudent kids.

The Sewing Lady also pushed around an old pram but this one was fitted with a hand-operated sewing machine. She did patching of sheets, pants, what have you. She would sit on an old box and turn the handle, and make a plain frock for 1s 6d. If you let her inside she did brisk business with the ladies. If no sewing offered she would do a charwoman's job and work for a few pence, or darn the old socks, or tackle other household jobs . . .

Then the woman swagger called Lou. She dressed like a man, went in the pub with the men, camped with a group of them. You could not tell Lou from a bloke except by her voice. Most likely she smelt like them too.

Also round Waimate roamed a Chinese swagger dressed in real Chinese fashion, dark baggy trousers, and a long plaited pigtail hanging to his waist. He pushed a small hand-cart, trying to sell his vegetables. Nobody knew where they came from. He slept with his cart. Kids reckoned that he was magic and made the veges under the moon. They never went near him unless they were in pairs. The route he travelled seemed to be Sheffield, Methven, Mayfield and the foothills.

SC 3

Happy Harry's trail was the same—he was a short fat man, his Christmas beard down to his waist. He did not excel as a worker, but would hoe and do similar light jobs for a snack and a shakedown. He was a loner, and would tell how his bedroll once went missing from his camp. Suspecting a fellow named Hayseed had swiped it, he spread a rumour among Hayseed's mates how poor suffering Happy Harry had actually died with the cold. Hayseed at the time was celebrating on the strength of a few bob accumulated from a few fencing and shed jobs. Well, stories have it that Happy Harry then camped in the local churchyard, expecting Hayseed to pass, and sure enough he did, in high spirits, wavering slowly along. Happy Harry just stood there, not a movement, not a word. Suddenly Hayseed saw him, thought he was seeing the ghost of poor old Happy Harry, and took off in great distress, crying: "I'd never have taken your roll if I'd known it would kill you!"

This Hayseed was a tall thin man, not frightened of work; he would tackle anything that came his way. He was noted for his bedroll and billy, and the fact that he always carried his own condensed milk, as milk was seldom given in the handout billy of tea. Hayseed liked his tea this way.

Shiny Bob (William Smith), from England originally, used to roam around the Coalgate-Sheffield area. He'd been a prospector before going on the swag and now he made a little money out of the coal he got. He'd found a little coalmine and used to dig it out with a pick and shovel, but the swaggers could never make out where he got his money from. He went out one day and never returned. A day and a night passed. His mates posted him as missing, and went out to look for him—they may have been swaggers, but still they were concerned about their mates. They trudged into the bush looking for Shiny Bob. They came across him, buried up to the neck with coal that he had picked out the day before, with one hand raised high and his old bald pate showing. That's what they saw.

When someone remarked on Bob's return to Glentunnel, he said: "Oh yes, turned up like a shiny bob" (shilling coin), and the name stuck. Among the first wounded in

World War One, he was on his way a second time when peace came.

Shiny Bob had coal dust in his blood, prospecting most of the Malvern hills, opening up several coalmines—the Klondyke at Homebush was the biggest—creating opportunities for others to make money, but never made much himself. He kept on fossicking to the day of his death, 11 February 1962, aged 81! He found antimony and bentonite, and searched round Picton for coal.

There was Hookey, a bloke with one arm and a hook on the other. A quiet man, he always stood in the shade, so you couldn't see his face; or he'd keep his face turned away from you and his head down. His area was around Weedons, Rolleston, the foothills of Sheffield, Mayfield, probably working south. Most people only saw him once, and never fullfaced. He was, it is said, very well mannered. (A wry veteran with a hook living round Taihape way had a different version for almost every enquiry when intrigued youngsters asked "How did you lose your hand?" Arthur Davis tells in a characteristic story. One reply went: "I was coming back from town with a pound of sausages when I went to sleep at the side of the road holding the sausages in one hand. When I woke up, a hungry dog had eaten almost up to my elbow.")

One old chap had a goat, and like Mary and her lamb, everywhere he went the goat went too. His invariable greeting: "Me throat's that dry—I could do with a good strong brew, lady"—the first time several countrywomen, quite impressed, had ever been called 'lady'. Billy, his reeking goat, was always given a crust of bread by Marion Trotter of Katiki, Palmerston, "although he really preferred chocolate biscuits and Christmas cake." From everything that was given to the old swagger, you can be sure that goat got his titbit. He led the goat on a chain and it was never out of his sight. He travelled the South Island. 'Goaty' had a tin for his tea. It is said his billy would turn a strong stomach. They reckon his billy tin smelt like a goat when hot water was put into it—and no wonder! because the goat used to drink the dregs when the old chap had finished with it.

The Musical Swagger [perhaps Freddy Ambrose?] roamed the Methven foothill stations, a small skinny man only about five feet tall with a bushy beard on a very small face. Said to be a good cook, he cooked a bit on the country stations.

After much persuasion from one husband, he showed the woman of the house how to dress and cook a sheep's head—delicious! He played a concertina and entertained the shearers and station hands in the evenings. He used to go in straight lines across country, cutting across the paddocks to various back-country stations, mostly at shearing time. Some say he was a religious old chap, always singing hymns of praise.

Many swaggers camped under the Kakanui or Kaikanui bridge. How they survived those cold South Island winters is anybody's guess. When in the Mayfield area they camped at Ruapuna Domain, Whiskers Blake's hideout.

Whiskers Blake was not exactly lovable: he was dirty, had a horse and dog, stole sheep (sixpence a head in Addington saleyards in 1933) for food and dog tucker, pinched hay for his horse.

Spud Murphy, very tall and stooped with a big nose and heavy slow brogue, also rode a horse, but usually with a foal at foot. What happened to each year's fresh foal nobody knew, most likely he sold it, and demanded the best stallion to cover his mare. Asked how he came by one seemingly well-bred foal, Murphy replied: "I slept under a gorse bush, next to a stud place in North Canterbury."

George Dundass saw him toss off in one great swig a medium glass of neat brandy at his father's Ida Valley Hotel one cold night in July, and remark: "That was a fine shandy gaff." (ie part lemonade part beer!).

Appearing again in Central Otago in an enormous military overcoat towards the end of World War One, he explained his two-year absence by saying he'd been in Trentham Camp, where the sergeant admonished him for not hitting the target once in three weeks.

" 'Sergeant,' I said, 'if I am here for the next three years, I will not hit that tarrgett.' I did not want to hit that bloddy tarrgett!" One chap thought he was a remittance man and last heard of him in the Blue Cliffs (St Andrews) area during the Second World War. Spud's circuit was always roving in the back country. He demanded shelter for his horse and foal. The cockies were a little afraid of him. Understandable—he was not a nice person.

For instance, a countryman saw him arrive just on dark at a station near the Lindis Pass: "He was not a popular caller, and his habits were so dirty that he had to sleep in coal sheds and so on.

"The boss made the justifiable excuse of all accommodation being taken up by musterers and shearers, and sent him on to the next place. There he was given somewhere to sleep, and when he came in for breakfast, the owner of that place brought it out to him, explaining he couldn't have it inside because ladies were there.

" 'And who might they be?'

" 'My wife, for one'.

" 'She can't be a bloody lady or she wouldn't have married you.' "

Mouthorgan Jack (not to be confused with mouth-organ playing John the Baptist) went till he dropped, found dead lying alongside a North Canterbury road.

> His rusted billy left beside the tree;
> Under a root, most carefully tucked away.
> His steel-rimmed glasses folded in their case
> Of mildewed purple velvet; there he lies
> In the sunny afternoon, and takes his ease,
> Curled like a possum within the hollow trunk.
> ... The roots and bones lie close among the soil,
> And he ascends in leaves towards the sky.

So Nancy Cate, in her 'The Dead Swagman'.

See also 'The Death Of The Hired Man', by Robert Frost which also includes:

> ... Home is the place where, when you have to go there,
> They have to take you in.

I should have called it
Something you somehow haven't to deserve.

Doing a bit of shearing, mostly dagging, Mouthorgan Jack used to get around the sheds, popular with his playing, and he also had a gramophone, ordering records from Christchurch. If he didn't like a record, he'd break it.

'Banjo' Paterson, the Australian poet who wrote 'Waltzing Matilda' and many other poems of station life, often mentioned 'swagmen', the Australian equivalent of our swaggers. By 1942 however, Australians we met in prisoner of war camps always referred to 'swagmen' as 'bagmen'.

In Paterson's poem, 'On Kiley's Run', he writes:

The swagman never turned away
With empty hand at close of day.

Further on in the poem, bad times come, and Kiley is forced to walk off the place. Ownership passes to an absentee owner in England and the name is changed to 'Chandos Park Estate'; Paterson records the change of climate as far as swagmen were concerned and says:

The lonely swagman in the dark
Must hump his swag past Chandos Park.

If you saw a figure in the distance with a jaunty walk and full pack up, here was Freddy Ambrose, stockily built, religious, disliking swear words. If the cook left, Fred would take over for a bit. He could lift a 200-pound bag and fling it across his shoulders. He later went to Woodstock, and when his hut there was burnt down moved to Oxford, the Salvation Army caring for him in his last days.

Some of Freddy's vigorous outback expeditions and river crossings have been wrongly attributed to John the Baptist, a less intrepid man who preferred the main roads and the beaten track.

Freddy Ambrose (cook at Glenrock 1924) quit Algidus because he reckoned the musterers there swore too much, according to Eric Baynon, shepherding then at Double Hill. He compared him with King Edward VII, beard and all!

He was what we could call 'partly-swagger', staying two to three months in a place.

Mountaineering when need be with a huge pack through flood, ice, snow, Freddy (Walter Fredrick Ambras, an Australian sailor coming ashore here about 1910) was almost "a minor Arawata Bill . . . something of a folk hero," considers Andrew Potter in *The Maorilander,* 1972.

"He attributed his fearlessness in the Alps and the furious rivers, to a small pocket-bible he always carried. He discovered and crossed Ambrose Saddle, high in the Rakaia peaks."

Delighting in playing his accordian and portable gramophone, this exceedingly tough, bearded old man died in 1970, aged 92, and might have been the cook, continues Potter, at the mid-Canterbury sheepstation where a shearer bawled in disgust from his tucker:

"Look at this bloody mutton, will yers!"

Irked at the language, the cook slapped down his pots and pans and prepared to depart.

"Ah, Jesus! I didn't mean it like that. I meant that it was bloody-well raw!"

Mollified the cook resumed work.

In the same issue, in a poem to him, 'the bearded swagger' of the kowhai country and mountain track, our balladeer Joe Charles says: *In my heart he lit a flame.*

Ambrose had a canvas bag like an Army kitbag, he'd put in all his clothes and gear, put it in the river (the bag had buoyancy), place his hands and chin on it, and kick himself along to the other side! Freddy had his silent days, when he would become upset at being stopped and spoken to.

"It's you, isn't it Fred?" said a backcountry man running into him in Blenheim in 1935.

"Yes," replied Freddy. "I remember you all right." Pause. Then: "Goodbye," and away he went.

A nickname of another seems to haunt: 'Jim the Whistler'— where are you, Jim? Who remembers? Only the name remains? Were you as happy as your name suggests? Or did this have a slightly sinister touch?

The Flying Scotsman, always in a hurry, stopped one day up-country and exclaimed: "I'll have to move fast. I won't get a feed around here. I will though if I make it to the valley," where the single men were camped during the depression—for the poor invariably looked after and sympathised with the poor in harsh times.

A gentle and courteous old man wellspoken and well-educated, who like the Flying Scotsman came regularly through the Waipara district, is not remembered half a century later by his name, but by his manners. When given a meal he would thank the cook gracefully, and in return offer to do the washing up, dishes, pots, and pans. Charlie, a rather similar old man with a goatee beard, rode a bike, and is remembered "because he really loved a game of cricket."

>Cycling Song
>*A bush full of*
>   *birds*
>*and a bag full of*
>   *barley.*
>*Over the ditch and*
>   *the moon*
>*went Charlie.*

Eric Dass mystified fellow travellers by writing out cheques; other swaggers couldn't make him out, and was Dass his real name? He was a cut above the others, not the hobo type, you'd never see Eric poorly dressed. He'd take off, vanish for some time, then like the homing pigeon return, the booze would flow for a while, then he'd be away again. Eric collapsed and died in the Rolleston hut, another remittance man gone west . . .

An engraver, Clocky, practised his art casually here and there when the mood took him, mostly repairing and overhauling clocks and watches, sharpening scissors and knives. Burgess may have been his real name. He could have been the man met by G. J. Nutsford when he himself was a swagger:

"He was an artist, at least his hobby was artistic.

"He would use a billy can a few times till it was nicely blackened by the fire and smoke, polish it, and with a needle scratch landscapes through the black to the shiny tin beneath. I understood these decorated billies were in demand."

Clocky ranged the countryside and the foothills pushing an old perambulator containing all his earthly possessions. One day to his anger and distress, his old pram was knocked over and damaged, the newspapers wrote this up, and Clocky got a new one. As time began to run out for him, he lived in an old clay cottage around the Annat district on the West Coast road.

Most of the swaggers carried very little with them: some carried a pot and billy, the bare necessities with little spare clothing. They seldom, if ever had a washing day—in case someone flogged the washing! They either knew nothing about body odour or couldn't smell it. But Goldtooth always had soap in his kit.

Goldtooth had a fortune in his mouth, a mouthful of gold teeth and crownings. He carried a full swag, and has been remembered in two areas, Rolleston and the foothills of Sheffield. He disappeared abruptly out of a shed one day when a shed hand swore he was going to pull out his teeth to make a few bob for the races. Apparently Goldtooth never spoke very much, and when he did he spoke with a plum in his mouth, perhaps a remittance man. He was well educated, a tall man, well dressed for a swagger, no bowyangs or holey boots. We may guess it was his first year out on the swag. He was a bit useless, and seems to have got the broomey jobs around the places—something easy.

Some swaggers of course never had a name, such as the old chap with a beard so long that he pulled it behind his back, from there brought it to his front, and tied it! There was no name for him, but once seen, never forgotten, the longest beard ever viewed around Canterbury, and maybe even the whole South Island.

Some of the swaggers were nicknamed by the cockies, some by the kids who used to cheek them on their way to school. Their real names were immaterial—no one was interested enough to want to know their names. Many were out of the nick; no jobs—depression. Times were hard, I'll say, ruddy hard, for everyone to survive.

St Peter was a weirdo. Everybody who knew him called the old cove St Peter. His main possession was an old bible with real dog-ears through thumbing. He was seen in Dunsandel and Rakaia. St Peter walked almost barefooted. He was tatty, his clothes nearly falling off him. His bowyangs kept his pants together. He seemed to cadge all his food at the doors of farmhouses. He was really down and out. A weasel-looking fellow, skinny and rough, his looks used to frighten hell out of the kids. He dossed down anywhere: hedges, haystacks, barns, old sheds—anywhere with a bit of cover from wind or rain or cold.

Elijah the Prophet haunted North Canterbury and surrounding districts where, when something stirred in his blood, he'd head like a hawk for a high point and begin preaching, to an audience of himself. On a still night his voice echoed far round the hills. Countryfolk who knew him would say: "He's at it again. Old Elijah—telling the Lord all about it."

Southbridge district to Collingwood on the Hook: that was the run of Paddy Murphy, the spud picker and odd-job man, working his way up and down North Canterbury, finally finishing by the rocks and caves at Tarakohe and the hairline blue horizon of Golden Bay. Paddy originally came from the Southbridge-Leeston district where he always returned, sometimes broke, sometimes in the money. His old boss willingly re-employed him when needs grew critical and would look after Paddy's money until it was nearly gone.

Then, after this short spell of living in leisure, Paddy would shoulder his roll and gear, and move on back north.

Paddy had one failing. He, by no means the only voyager to founder on this rock, had one hell of a lot of trouble getting past the Rat Trap, the innocent looking little pub nestled so strategically at the top of the long valley leading to Takaka. A trap indeed, once the perilous Takaka Hill lies behind the tremulous traveller.

It catches them both ways.

At one time Paddy did a bit of work on the Cobb power project set at the end of a miniature-type Buller Gorge road, and if he somehow managed to get past the Trap, he would hightail for Southbridge and again live in leisure, pay any debts and booze up, until he was skinned.

A swagger named Barney the Bull did a lot of gorsecutting, a real worker. One day he played a prank. He flogged a sheet off somebody's line, dolled himself up in it, and set off biking to the camp at the Selwyn bridge to scare hell out of the rest of the swaggers. However, riding his bike all sheeted like this, he got tangled up in the bike chain and wheels, and head over tip went Barney the Bull. Sheets were strong in those days, he couldn't get himself out of it; besides he probably was a few sheets in the wind himself, and a teamster had to help him out of his predicament. When asked how the blazes he got himself into this mess, he told the teamster of his intention to terrify the swaggers camped at the bridge by appearing as a ghost.

Barney the Bull always carried blankets and a spare suit of clothes. He was nicknamed Barney the Bull because of the lavish stories he told, and he really laid it on! He mostly biked everywhere, and he wasn't an alky, like most of the others. He stood about six foot four, had a beard and scraggy hair. He covered Waimate and Methven areas.

A man and his dog: an old chappie, with his dog called Scott, were seen in the Springfield area, a real hard case, but he would chop wood or do gardening. When food was given to him he then asked for a little for Scott. His dog was an old beardie-looking animal, near enough like him. He would feed the dog food given to him, but if the dogtucker wasn't good he would throw it away contemptuously. This old swagger wanted paper and envelopes if the missus could spare them, because he wrote regularly to a son who never knew that his father swagged. He carried one of those gladstone bags. He unlocked it carefully, put the paper and envelopes inside, and locked it up. Nobody knew what else he had in there, perhaps money for stores. He was a sort of Love-me-love-my-dog sort of chappie.

A wizzled-up old fellow had a face like an old potato.

He had an old dapple grey horse called Horace, about as old as himself which never ran or trotted, it just walked. He carried his bedding in a black blanket and several old sacks sewn together. I am told he was too old to work, but would put a mender in a pot or pan for one penny. If he scrubbed and polished the pot as well he would charge threepence, but if you gave him a cup of tea, and solids, he would charge one penny. He always thanked the housewife most politely, and loved to tell stories to the kids or sing them his only song *Michael Finnigan,* and play his flat mouth organ: 'Poor old Michael Finnigan, He grew whiskers on his chinagin, The wind came out and blew them innagin, Poor old Michael Finnigan—Beginagin . . .' He would have the kids walking home from school singing this.

Harry Mamos (Alf Heisingbuttel), was born near Christchurch in the Marshland district. Not too much was known about him in his early days. He eventually moved to the Rolleston-West Melton district and would never stroll very far. Old Harry had a very keen sense of smell. One trick of his was to flog the meths while the woman of the house had her back turned getting him something to eat and a cup of tea. If there were two bottles of meths, one would be gone. Instead of getting stuck into his handouts, Harry would sneak back and have a guzzle at the remaining bottle. He was caught at this with the bottle up to his mouth. How many housewives I wonder lost their meths like this?

Jimmy Robinson used to do the country pubs around Darfield way before joining up with the Rolleston gang. He was killed there on a Christmas morning, the previous night sleeping in long grass by the railway track after celebrating Christmas Eve with too much enthusiasm.

Arthur Brunt studied law but tossed it in to take to the swag, tall with long white whiskers. Arthur had a pair of riding pants given to him, and, with his socks pulled up over the top, when he walked and you saw him from behind, he looked like a flamingo walking. He had long spindly legs.

Arthur, having a row with a cocky, exclaimed: "I won't come back till I'm 100 years old!" In a year, he was back.

Ray Kirk's 'Who's Who' 39

"What brought you back so soon?" asked the cocky.

"Absence makes the heart grow fonder," replied Arthur. (Was he the Arthur Sutton Brunt, died Old Men's Home, Ashburton, aged 82, on 12.4.40?)

Bill Harrison walked around waving his arms about, talking to himself and saying: "All the land around me was mine, but they ratted it from me."

Another swagger uneasy in mind was Paddy Reilly, a ship's cook, shipwrecked twice off the coast of Japan. This disturbed his mind. He'd get plonked and go into the dingbats. He did relieving-cook jobs on the stations.

Scotty Gilmore: A quiet old bloke, roaming modestly here and there, little known about him.

Bob McLagan, always looking for a likely touch, for a loan of half a crown for his entrance fee into the pub. Once in, he was right!

Ted Tanner started swagging on a bike, had a violin, and I presume played in country pubs, knocking out tunes to the delight of the crowd. Methven-Timaru-Waimate.

Seemingly, Russian Jack survived on hen eggs, hunting in the early morning for stray nests, then taking all eggs found to the blacksmith (Mr Riley at Methven?) where he cooked them hard. Not to be confused with Wairarapa's Russian Jack, this Methven swagger is said to have fled across Siberia with three cobbers who fell by the wayside. Jack jumped ship in Auckland and later, in 1932, was blamed for 'the bomb incident' in the 1932 Auckland riots.

Flash Fancy mainly worked in the woolsheds, well educated, spent his money on flash clothes and booze, hence the name. Fancy nearly got himself married by asking a middle-aged woman if he could lay his bones by her bones. She considered his flight of fancy to be a proposal—took him a month of hard talking to get out of it! Poor old Fancy was in a real flap!

John Barleycorn worked in the sheds, etc; known for his tall stories (were they all tall, though?) which kept people spellbound. One of the great bull artists of the day.

Tim Cane (Gentleman Jim) had a bike, but used to walk alongside it because he didn't want to wear out the tyres. He was a gentleman, clean and tidy, tall, thin, whitehaired, bearded.

He would go around cutting wood for a helping of morning tea, and if asked for dinner would work all the harder, chopping a big pile of wood and washing thoroughly, using plenty of soap, before coming inside for a meal. He was a reserved type of man and never mixed very much with the others who passed through. At one time he had a bach or shack on one of the farms around the place. He was at Rolleston for awhile.

An old identity named Old Bob, not a swagger, carted Gentleman Jim around occasionally on a pubcrawl. This day they were returning home under the weather, the two of them in the cart with heads over the side like a couple of bags of spuds. When the kids coming home from school spotted them, they let fly with handfuls of stones.

"We better get home, Jim, it's hailing like beggary," bellowed Old Bob.

When drunk, all of a sudden Old Bob would go religious: "My head is bending low—my head is bending low. I have made peace with the Lord." Away he would go. Another swig out of the old gallon jar and then out would come his crumbfilled mouth organ to play a 'real easy' as he called it: *The Irish Washerwoman*.

Returning to Gentleman Jim, the swagger. In his later years he lived in a hut up the Bealey Road with a friend. I understand he passed on about 1962. Rumoured to be worth a few bob when he died.

There was Old Jack, living in the country area where a threshing mill was based. He worked on the mill, saved his earnings and made them last until next season by swagging. He always seemed to find an easy way to travel. He went to Christchurch in the cold weather of June, July and August, his hut empty until the spring.

Fishy was the only swagger I have heard of who carried a fishing line wherever he went, and pulled a little handcart decorated with fishes painted on it. He had a wire under the cart to carry his bedroll. He would fish in the rivers, catch only as many as he could sell, and then traipse around selling his fish cheap to keep his custom. He fished where there were small settlements, a lean man, with glasses, said to make his own flies, which he would sell for a penny.

And to end our beat for the day: Paddy the Pig's main home was a hole in a haystack. He had a good friend in a hotel landlady who gave him what was left after the patrons were fed. Always wore a cap, a strong man.

Said to have never missed church, Paddy the Pig would sneak in when all were seated, kneel at the back of the church, then sneak out before the service had finished . . .

Violet Kerr Meets 'The Shiner':
An Immortal Swagger

When we were asked at school what famous person we would like to meet, all the nice little kids answered dutifully: "King George V", "Queen Mary", "Sir Charles Fergusson". I wasn't nice. I said "The Shiner!"

When the teacher, ignorant creature, inquired: "And who is The Shiner?" and was told, "A swagger," she coldly turned away, and ever after, I felt, regarded me with a certain distaste.

I am happy to say I *did* meet The Shiner, and this was the highlight of my young life.

I was born at Maheno, in North Otago, where my father was a struggling dairy farmer—dairying, cropping, Clydesdale breeding, and, his greatest love, the breeding of Standard breds.

Our farm was a lovely place, winding through it the Island Stream between heavily-wooded banks, where, along with the willow, poplar, native trees and flax, small orchards appeared of apple and plum trees.

In some places the stream became shallow, sliding round little islands covered thick with mint and wild raspberry canes, with those old-fashioned, honey-sweet, golden-coloured raspberries never seen nowadays. In deep shadowy pools trout rings rippled on still summer evenings. The stream bank was a favourite camping place for The Shiner.

The farm would have been a lovely place to have grown up in, but unfortunately while I was still quite small, my father's ill-health forced him to sell up. We moved to a small property near Dunedin. I carried with me memories of the stream, of the wide acres of green oats bending before the wind, and of the animals. But in spite of my vivid six year old memories of the Island Stream farm, I couldn't remember much about The Shiner, although I must have seen him often at harvest time. Perhaps I was too busy following in my father's footsteps, for horses seemed to have left more impression than humans.

But after we left Maheno, my parents talked a great deal about The Shiner, especially my mother, who had known him when she was young. Of all the quaint, colourful characters my mother had known in the early days, The Shiner fascinated her the most.

Imagine then my delight when I did meet The Shiner when I was much older—a teenager. Although it is now over 40 years since that meeting, the picture of him is still clear. I'm quite sure my memory has played no tricks.

The Shiner was tall—a good, well built figure, carrying no spare flesh, and with a flat tummy, in spite of all the liquid refreshment he was so fond of! He must have been getting on in years, too, but looked fresh and youthful. My memory of his face: pleasant, good-natured looking, dark, clean-shaven, neat featured. I would say his face was oval in shape, rather broad across the cheek-bones, with rounded, apple-cheeks, and, of course, heavily tanned and reddened by the weather.

He was soberly dressed, clean and tidy, wearing a felt hat (my mother could remember him often wearing three straw hats stacked one above the other), a grey striped shirt, dark waistcoat and pants, and heavy boots, yellowed by the dust of the road. The Shiner's voice was pleasant, quiet and inclined to drawl. The drawl, according to my mother, was most pronounced when Ned was putting across one of his tall stories, or trying to talk himself out of a tight corner.

I have never yet come across anyone with a photograph of The Shiner. *Surely* someone would have photographed such a wellknown person.

I was told how The Shiner had arrived very late one night at our farm, asking could he please sleep in the shed? My mother and her sister, then only young girls, were alone and were very much surprised at The Shiner's manner. Normally cheerful and chatty, this night he was quite different: morose, and peculiarly inclined to take offence where none was intended.

My grandfather, who then owned the farm, had a very warm spot for The Shiner, and always allowed him to help himself to fruit from the orchard, but that night The Shiner had asked, hesitantly and pathetically, if he could have apples and mushrooms? The girls had never seen him in such an odd mood.

The reason?

Later they heard how he had just been thrown out of a neighbour's house by Maggie, the Scotswoman, for cheating at cards during a game in the kitchen, and had come across to our farm seeking a shakedown with rather ruffled feelings. Maggie must have got over her indignation fairly quickly, for soon she and The Shiner were on good terms again.

Maggie, in her way, was certainly a colourful character, too. Her name was McKay, and she kept house for her brother Jock whose farm was near Maheno township. Jock, by the way, had a large pet sheep which chewed tobacco! When Jock had a chew, the sheep demanded its share.

Maggie was a handsome, black-eyed, energetic woman who loved feeding people.

Swaggers never left McKay's door with a mere handout. They were all taken in for a sit-down meal. The Shiner however was the only swagger I ever heard of who was invited to stay for weeks. During one of these lengthy stays, he 'blotted his copybook' by cheating at cards, and Maggie, who in spite of her kindness had a stormy temper, boxed his ears thoroughly and threw him out, a nasty experience for The Shiner, suddenly having to take to the road late at night with the prospect of sleeping on chaffsacks, after the comforts of McKay's guest room.

Maggie McKay seemed to have been wellknown for her outbursts of temper, which subsided as quickly as they flared up. My father used to laugh reminiscently about 'Maggie's tantrums'. Perhaps The Shiner would not find it so difficult to creep back to the McKay fold after the storm was over, although according to my mother, Maggie was said to be very watchful ever after when playing cards with The Shiner.

When The Shiner was young, he had been a familiar figure at the old Caledonian Sports Meetings, held in Oamaru at New Year time. Here, he always competed in the Irish jig, and became wellknown for spectacular double shuffles and back-skips. Enthusiastic cheers always greeted his appearance, and people who knew him well became angry when the judges did not place The Shiner among the winners. However, The Shiner in his everyday clothes (probably three straw hats on his head and a red handkerchief round his neck) could scarcely have been considered correctly attired among the earnest competitors.

A neat trick The Shiner played during the days before the First World War, was told to me with enjoyment by a relative. The Artillery used to practise in the hills beyond Maheno, on the late Colonel Nicholl's Kuriheka Station. Quantities of feed were needed in camp for the horses, and one day when a battery was on its way up to the hills, the officer spotted a stack of hay handy to the road. The farmer had just walked round the side of the haystack, so the officer, quick to sieze a good opportunity, promptly rode over to ask him if he would consider selling the hay? The farmer agreed, and pointing out its exceptionally good quality, promptly received a good price for it on the spot. A waggon pulled into the paddock, and preparations went ahead for removing the stack.

Everyone was satisfied—that is, until a very angry man arrived, demanding to know what the blazes was happening to his haystack? The officer was having difficulty in convincing the rightful owner that he had just bought the stack, when the farmer suddenly remembered that The Shiner had camped there the night before!

Of The Shiner himself there was no sign. He was well on his way, with his ill-gotten gains, heading joyfully for the nearest pub.

Another 'Shiner' story concerns a Canterbury runholder who was trying to sell his property. The stock and station agent to whom he had entrusted his business was not having too much success. Then the runholder received the cheering news that a prospective buyer was on his way—a wealthy Australian grazier, very interested in purchasing a New Zealand property.

In due course, the agent arrived with the prospective buyer, and the runholder received him with relief and delight. The buyer looked a typical Aussie: lean, weather-beaten, cheerful. He was somewhat loud in his dress, with his boldly checked jacket, but there was no doubt about it, he was interested in the run. All he wanted was a bit of time to look round and make up his mind.

Full of hope, the runholder threw open his home to the Aussie, and whisky flowed like water. Time passed. The agent became restless, then impatient. He began to push the Aussie for a decision. Finally, the Aussie was forced to make up his mind.

Yes, he admitted, this was just the place he was looking for. All that remained now was the trifling matter of signing papers and paying for the property. With more good cheer, the men parted with arrangements made to meet again at the office of a certain Timaru solicitor. On the appointed day, the runholder and the agent arrived, but there was no sign of the Australian. They waited, but he never came. Nor did they ever see him again.

The rascally Shiner was back in North Otago, his borrowed plumes, the checked jacket, returned to its owner with whom he had a bet (which of course, he had won), by his successful pose as the Australian buyer. Into the bargain, he had enjoyed plenty of good food and drink.

Understandably, many must have regarded The Shiner as a shameless parasite, but for every one who condemned him for his vagabond ways, there seemed to be scores of others who forgave him his frailties, and accepted as gifts the colour and laughter he brought to their sober, uneventful day.

My father had a Shiner story, which apparently had been told with glee by The Shiner himself.

Ned had been given the job of digging a well. He put in an honest day's toil and dug down more than six feet, before he stopped work for the night. Next morning, returning to the well, he was dismayed to find that the walls had fallen in. This was more than The Shiner had bargained for. He immediately sought a solution to his problem.

Removing his hat and coat, he laid them beside the well, then collecting his pick and shovel, Ned retired to a secluded spot in some nearby bushes. There he rested in comfort, until he heard approaching footsteps.

Then The Shiner called faintly: "Help! Help . . .!"

There were gratifying sounds of consternation, hurrying footsteps, the clink of shovels, then (and this must have been music to The Shiner's ears) the sounds of frenzied digging.

When the rascally Ned judged that his 'rescuers' would have cleared the well down to where he had left off the night before, he emerged from his hiding place.

He stared at the concerned toilers, surprised, asking what was wrong? He hadn't got much sleep the night before (explained The Shiner), so he'd drifted off into the bushes for a bit of a lie down and rest before starting work. Funny, but he must have fallen asleep . . . must have had a bit of a nightmare, too . . . hmmmm . . . didn't know that he'd called out in his sleep though!

My grandfather had always employed The Shiner at harvest time, and regarded him as a good worker, but others had found him unreliable, walking out abruptly and leaving them shorthanded in the middle of harvesting.

In his younger days, The Shiner seemed to have been much the same as the other young men—he had enjoyed talking and joking with the girls, and there had been noisy and genial arguments when the harvesters gathered at mealtimes.

Any young single girl who proved herself a good cook, invariably received an offer of marriage from The Shiner.

My aunt was a good hand at making plum duff, so The Shiner announced his intentions of marrying her. One day at dinner a little later she reminded him: "Ned, I thought you wanted to marry me."

If she imagined The Shiner would have any difficulty in talking himself gracefully out of that, she was in error. He looked suitably innocent, then drawled gently and pityingly:

"Oh, you have made a mistake—it wasn't you I asked. It was the other one."

Fortunately for The Shiner, the 'other one', the younger sister, wasn't at home at the time, and he succeeded in raising a laugh at my aunt's expense.

But if some members of my family regarded 'old Ned' with tolerance and liking, my mother's stepmother had little sympathy for him. When The Shiner came up from his camp beside the Island Stream one morning at milking time, asking for a billy for milk, he was told to help himself from a nearby bucket of fresh milk.

My grandmother, expecting him to fill his billy by pouring the milk from the bucket, was justifiably enraged when she caught him in the act of dunking a very dirty black billy into her clean bucket of milk. Even the inside of the billy was dirty. A fiery-tempered little Scotswoman, my grandmother practically chased The Shiner over to the creek where she made him clean the billy thoroughly.

She then made sure that the milk was poured from bucket to billy, and not bailed out.

"Dirty old de'il!" was how grandmother summed up The Shiner.

Yes: I can still remember every detail of that day we met The Shiner on the Brockville road which ran up through what was then a farming district, at the back of Dunedin. I can still hear my mother's sudden, delighted exclamation of "There's The Shiner!"

More than ten years had passed since we had left the farm and the stream in North Otago, but The Shiner's memory was good, remembering various members of the family and recalling incidents.

He asked with a touch of sadness if my mother ever heard any news of Maggie McKay—the little Scotswoman who had chased him out of the house for cheating at cards, and who had fed him so generously. Maggie, too, had left North Otago.

After her brother's death, she married a sheep farmer and went to live in the North Island. The Shiner listened eagerly to the little bits of news. He had not forgotten Maggie and her brother, or their kindness to him.

That day of our meeting near Dunedin, The Shiner had come from the north, through Dunedin, and was heading for the Taieri Plain. We watched him walk away into the afternoon sunshine, his tall figure bent against the steepness of the hill road. For a long time afterwards we used to talk about "the day we met The Shiner."

If The Shiner could come back today, he would find Brockville a strange, alien place, for the quiet little green farms have gone. The orchards and the farmhouse gardens with their lilacs and redhot pokers have vanished, and the friendly white road that wound uphill between the pines and blue gums, the stone walls and high thorn hedges, is lost forever under the tangled tarsealed streets running between the endless red brick bungalows of the raw-looking housing settlement.

When age took its toll of The Shiner's strength, he became an inmate of the Old Men's Home in Tyne Street, Oamaru, whose comfortable citizens often saw him wandering up and down the street, a lonely old man without kin or friends.

I hope that somewhere The Shiner found a happier land of unchanging rural scenes, where in some friendly Celestial pub he met again all his old mates of the open road, and that once again he and Maggie can enjoy a quiet game of cards.

Two Shiners

My favourite story about The Shiner is not about his gift for seeing and seizing an opportunity, his humorous tricks and deceptions, although we all delight in officialdom and assured smugness getting a good jolt in the ribs: "This happen *to me?* It's . . . it's . . . positively *undignified!*"
No.
My favourite story came through Bob Smith of Kawerau, who told how The Shiner, a considerable toiler when inclined, was working for J. B. Reid of Elderslie when suddenly he quit.
Reid protested the harvest was only beginning.
The Shiner explained a seagull had just flown overhead saying:
"South, Shiner! South!"
Reid understood . . .

"Where are you going now, Mr Slattery?" little Alan J. McKenzie asked him respectfully, as the tall lanky traveller washed the white handkerchief he wore round his neck in the Awamoa Creek, Oamaru, close to a double row of macrocarpa trees, where horses and swaggers took shelter.
"Don't know, lad. I just think I'll follow the swallows."

John A. Lee, incapable of writing a dull sentence, carried the swag himself briefly in his youth ("The Starlight Boarding House Fraternity") and in his books recorded and preserved the swagger with a loving glow, rather like some insect held within a golden hunk of kauri gum. Without John our swaggers, particularly his endearing favourite The Shiner, could well have trailed away and vanished over the hill. Trudge through the deserts of most of our provincial histories: seldom if ever a merry or morose swagger on the horizon, or a human heartbeat, for that matter. The writers are enthralled with station owners, vestry meetings, city councillors, hungry tradesmen, boroughs and boards, snuffling not the dust and sweat of everyday simple people's lives, but the dust of annual reports and newspaper files and passenger lists of The First Ships.

One district historian—see him plump and plush, thumbs in armholes of waistcoat, rocking on his heels—wrote:

"Prosperity and the war of 1914-18 removed this curious population from the roads."

Another district historian waved them aside, as if with a petulant feather duster, with the word 'eccentrics'.

Ned (Edward) Slattery, to give him his real name, a tall, lively, neat (when he wished) man in his early thirties, came out to New Zealand from Ireland's County Clare in 1869, to take to the roads of our far south, from Gore to around Timaru.

Trapped between the perfidious English of Christchurch and the dour porridge of Dunedin, shackled by the sea to the east and the Alps to the west, the poor Irish fought and boozed and worshipped their strange technicolour idols at Temuka, Fairlie and round Timaru, with Oamaru a sort of No Man's Land welcoming the new century with at least 20 brothels, especially active at haymaking, harvesting, and shearing, regardless of further backaches.

The Little Sisters of the Poor looked after him in the last grey, rather sad days, before he died and was buried in Andersons Bay Cemetery, Dunedin, in 1927.

Appearance? Ivan Patterson of Dunedin saw him as "tall and rather slim, hat with rim turned down, what in those days was called a Doctor Jim hat. I passed him on the roads a few times in the early 1920s but cannot recall him with a billy or swag. He often carried a small stick, perhaps a willow twig.

"Others remember him with a stick over his shoulder and at its end a small bundle tied in a large red and white spotted handkerchief or scarf.

"He was an Irishman through and through, had the Irish

sense of humour, and although I never saw it, I could well imagine he had the Irish temper if roused."

A man reputed to be related to The Shiner was John Slattery, of Morven, South Canterbury. He apparently disapproved strongly of The Shiner's way of life—but South Canterbury seemed to be right on the swagger's regular route.

I think the first yarn I heard about The Shiner told of him taking a crockery demijohn into the pub to be filled with draught whisky, when it was cheap and plentiful. This done, he remarked airily:

"Just charge that to my account," and began to depart.

"Oh no you don't, Shiner!" exclaimed the publican, grabbing the container back and with a flourish emptying its contents into the whisky barrel. "I've been had too often by you."

"You're a hard man," grumbled The Shiner, departing crestfallen to behind the nearest hedge, to joyously break open the demijohn and squeeze a number of very satisfying drams out of a very large sponge he'd popped inside previously.

Similarly, and again the time and the place and the barman had to be chosen with care and discretion, he walked into the bar with a half-filled whisky bottle, and told the new barman "to be so good as to fill it up, my man."

Then The Shiner began to make off, waving a reassuring hand and saying in his best voice he'd return tomorrow to square up.

"Not on your life! No fear. I'm not that green!" responded the new barman quickly, nipping out to grab the bottle, and when still no cash appeared, tipping half of the bottle back, while The Shiner stood by disgustedly, rumbling about bad manners, cold hearts and man's inhumanity to man . . .

Leaving the pub and on his way, at the first private and sheltered spot, he would proceed to enjoy a boozeup from his precious bottle of cold tea and free whisky.

The Shiner chanced to be passing a hotel in South Canterbury just as the proprietor was opening the door at 9 a.m., (tells

Two Shiners

Ivan Patterson). Seeing The Shiner, the publican called cheerily:

"Good morning, Ned!"

The Shiner cupped his hand to his ear and said: "I beg your pardon?" The hotelkeeper again bid him good morning, whereupon The Shiner said: "Many thanks boss, but it must be only a small one, as it's a bit early in the day."

Foxed, the hotelkeeper invited The Shiner in and asked what would he have?

"A whisky please."

No bowsers and meticulous measures then, you helped yourself from the bottle, which is just what The Shiner did, filling the tumbler to the very brim, downing the drink in one great swallow, thanking the boss warmly, then walking out into an even better morning . . .

Two publicans in Central Otago were deadly rivals. Approaching one of them, The Shiner, ordering a large whisky and a pint of beer, asked casually:

"I wonder, do you accept stamps?"

"I do, yes."

"Good."

The Shiner scoffed his drinks and ordered a repeat.

"Hey now. Half a mo'—where are your so-and-so stamps?"

"Certainly. How many do you want?"

"Six will do for a start."

The Shiner began pounding a boot noisily on the floor, ponderously counting as he thumped.

Irked, and preparing to throw the swagger out, the publican suddenly saw the funny side, grinned, and said confidentially:

"Tell you what. Look here: if you can put that trick across the so-and-so at the other pub, you can have all you want to drink for the night."

The Shiner lifted his swag, entered the other pub, and successfully repeated the performance.

The publican's reaction was the same as his rival's—and The Shiner stayed in the town gloriously drunk for two days.

He did drink tea, however, and arriving late for midday dinner at a St Bathan's home, by the time he'd finished the substantial second course the tea had cooled. The housewife apologised:

"I'm sorry the tea isn't as hot as it should be."

Ned replied: "And a cold stomach won't *warrrm* it."

When in the neighbourhood of Oamaru, The Shiner pricked up his ears upon hearing that the parish priest, not in the best of health, had been advised to drink goats' milk. But a suitable goat was hard to find.

Beaming, The Shiner appeared at the priest's place (records Kay Fleming in the *Weekly News* 14 September, 1972) with the good news he'd got a goat all right, a fine one, a picture of health and goodwill, now tied up to the front gate.

"Splendid," said the priest, gladly handing over two pounds and, as he was rather preoccupied at the time, telling The Shiner to take the goat round to the orchard and tether it in a good spot.

That evening the housekeeper returned from the orchard saying she couldn't milk the goat.

Resignedly the priest said he supposed he'd just have to do it himself.

"You'll find it very difficult," said the housekeeper. "You see, that goat's a billy."

Oamaru has a painting of The Shiner, and surely one day will raise a statue to him, a sort of elderly Peter Pan of the Roads? As a T.V. star he was a hit early in 1976.

King George V Park, when covered with clumps of flax and scrub, was used for shelter by the wandering ones—the vagrants or itinerants—who if alive today, would gape astonished at an actual painting (based on an old sketch) of The Shiner displayed in the Oamaru Licensing Trust Brydone Hotel. What a contrast with the grog-shops and doss-houses they knew, concentrated about Tyne and Thames Streets, or Humber and Ribble Streets.

The Shiner, with Professor Barney White Rats, rightly make their appearance in *History of North Otago from 1853*, an Antipodean 'Under Milk Wood' collection of pioneers memories published by the *Oamaru Mail*. Two oldtimers,

Two Shiners

now quoted here, contributing how The Shiner got a meal, his Irish jig, strategic patches, and his greyhounds:

It is probably no exaggeration to say The Shiner was New Zealand's champion in getting a free meal, and for guile and blarney he had few equals.

Heading for Kurow just before midday he pointed to a house and asked:

"Who lives over there?"

"That's Mrs So and So," said his friend, "but it's no use going there. They've never been known to give anyone a bite."

"Oh well," drawled out Ned, "there's no harm in trying," so he knocked on the door.

"Good morning, lady," he commenced. "What a lovely garden you have, and such beautiful flowers. You must know a lot about gardening. I never saw such fine blooms before, it is the greatest show in the Colony."

This eloquent introduction naturally made a favourable impression, and Ned could see he was creating the right atmosphere. Just then, the small son of the house came to the door and this gave Ned a further opportunity for his complimentary references.

"What a fine lad, what a bright little chap," he said, and with this he pulled a shilling out of his pocket and handed it to the child. The little boy was delighted and the mother thought what a nice generous man the visitor was. With these preliminaries over, Ned said that he would have to be going as he thought of calling upon Mr . . . . down the road about a mile, and having dinner there.

"Why not have dinner with us? We would be pleased if you would," said the lady. Ned demurred but then consented. Needless to say he did justice to the generous spread placed before him. Dinner over, he rose from the table, and moved to the door, at the same time calling to the little boy, who was still tossing the shilling around.

"Let me have a look at that coin," he said. The boy handed him the money and Ned remarked:

"I think sonny, you've been playing with it long enough."

With this he quietly returned the shilling to his pocket, bade the woman good-day: "You've a lovely garden here."

He knew every road and byroad, barn and doss-house in every county from Gore to Timaru. At harvest time he always made for Oamaru and surrounding districts. New Year would generally find him competing in the Irish jig at the old Caledonian meetings: "Dancing a good jig, his appearance cheered, the crowd demanding his famous double shuffle and back skips, [then] carrying him off to Micky Doyle's booth at the side of the old grandstand to drink his health in the old lead pots . . ."

One day Ned was sewing large patches on the knees of his trousers when another knight of the road chanced to come upon him.

"Whatever are you putting patches on the knees of your pants for, they are not worn out?"

The Shiner looked up at his friend and asked him to turn around.

"I thought so," said The Shiner, "you won't get many jobs: you've got your patches on the wrong place."

The Shiner was very fond of greyhounds and for many years his sole companions were a pair of these dogs which shared his fortunes on the broad highway.

His memory was excellent. Mr Sinclair, head shepherd at Maraweka Station, had a young schoolboy son, whom The Shiner once saw. Years later The Shiner, walking down the street in Oamaru, met the son Jimmy Sinclair, stopped to talk, and asked after his father. Jimmy, incidentally, after a variety of jobs, worked for David Gunn of Hollyford, was leading guide for the Martins Bay track, then a labourer in the Hillside Workshops, and died a few years ago in a house in South Dunedin with only his dogs to mourn him.

A country newspaper editor of the far south and later in the Wairarapa, Arthur Vile, during his time in Oamaru met The Shiner when "we were making a motor trip to the country. A long slab of six feet, with unkempt hair and something like a turban round his head, he carried a little parcel over his shoulder which could not have weighed more than ten pounds, and which contained the whole of his earthly possession.

"His feet were covered with a pair of heavy leather boots, laced with stout string, which had the appearance of long usage, but which had never come into contact with a brush from the day they were bought.

"How he came by his name I was never able to ascertain. He was a hobo who had been on the roads for fully half a century, and it is estimated that in that time he walked at least 100,000 miles.

"The Shiner was said to have had quite an interesting career in his youth and his intelligence was well above average.

"Whether it was women, or commerce, or family disruption that induced him to come to the Dominion and follow the nomadic life, need not be discussed. It is sufficient to say that he was a man of the roads whose personality attracted a great deal of attention, who was seldom permitted to leave a station or farmstead empty-handed, and who never refused to cut a bit of firewood if asked."

Around noon, during the general election of 1919, Ivan Patterson, deputy returning officer at Waitaki polling booth, on the border of South Canterbury and Otago, "heard heavy sounds of footsteps coming into the booth, and a very tall man with a slightly hooked nose walked up to the table. In a loud voice he told us his name was Edward Slattery, and asked me if he was on the roll. He was.

"We were now to be entertained by the famous Shiner."

Armed with ballot papers and asking (as a voter is entitled to) for assistance and information about recording his vote, The Shiner "let off a torrent of abuse at candidate A, then let drive at candidate B, his remarks not at all complimentary."

Who would he vote for?

"That's no business of yours!"

As for voting on the liquor trade, he told Patterson all prohibition people should be hanged from the nearest lamp post.

"After this The Shiner impartially proceeded to give me a lecture on the evils of drink.

"I said he could not express his private opinions in the booth. He said he thought he could vote without assistance now. He recorded his vote, folded up the ballot papers in the correct manner, and placed them in the right boxes. He gave us all a big smile and expressed his thanks, retiring from the booth. The old scamp was having me on, because at the end of the day there were no informal votes to be counted, so he must have recorded his vote correctly.

"The Shiner simply couldn't resist having a joke or playing a prank, usually for his own benefit and at the expense of the other person."

Time inevitably took its toll. The last time Ned Slattery passed through Mosgiel he looked very ill and had boils on his neck.

I began wondering, as our book took shape, if the publishers and I could use money from the royalties (hopefully!) to get at least a modest stone placed over the unmarked pauper's grave of The Shiner; with luck, someone later might run to an apt and endearing little wayside statue, you never can tell.

Woe and alas . . .

Apparently some years ago, the Dunedin City Council gave permission to someone to put a headstone on another pauper's grave at Andersons Bay. The headstone went up, but soon a relation of another pauper tucked away in the same grave objected, demanding the removal of the headstone. This person probably complained in true New Zealand fashion this wasn't a fair go, marking only one name of those gathered below. Anyhow the headstone was removed.

Similarly, Edward Slattery, died 11 August 1927, aged 89, does not lie alone in Lot 95 Block 25. Three other adults and two children were buried in the same grave. If a headstone arose for Edward Slattery, you bet relatives, friends, or descendants of the collection in the same plot would be complaining of discrimination.

Two Shiners

The easy companionship of the road does not extend to a city's graveyard.

"I think," soothingly wrote D. M. Shirley, Town Clerk, "it would be better if you were to let the matter rest."

But we have pictures and echoes of another Shiner—a Southlander—thanks to Wallace R. Hall of Edendale, and his mother who was born at Mataura in 1889. This now is what Wallace wrote to me:

One of the last of the Southland swaggers—if not the very last—was Larry, or Dave, Sinclair. Because he followed the same 'profession' as the wellknown Ned Slattery of Otago and South Canterbury, old Larry was sometimes referred to as the Shiner, but if anyone said this to his face, in a very surly voice he would reply:

"My name's not Shiner!"

Apparently, he resented comparisons.

Larry would tell people that he had started on the roads at the age of ninteen which would be somewhere around 1890, and he continued swagging until he was well into his eighties. I think he died in the Old Men's Home at Riverton sometime in the 1950s.

Apart from the fact that it was his own wish, there seemed to be no reason why he should spend his whole life tramping the roads. Apparently he came from a well-to-do family. His sister, who had married a prominent businessman in Invercargill, would periodically outfit him with new clothes. No doubt he was somewhat of an embarrassment to his sister, and the story is told of at least one occasion when Larry was enjoying a meal in his sister's kitchen when some flash visitors arrived at the front door. She had to hustle old Larry unceremoniously out the back door before going to admit her visitors at the front.

Larry was not likely to be pleased at this kind of treatment either. He was very easily offended. On his country rounds he treated people as if they should feel very honoured to have him calling on them. During World War Two when certain foodstuffs were rationed, Larry told one woman:

"People don't seem to be as pleased to see me as they once were."

A few years earlier, during the depression, Larry told the same lady that he always tried to call on people who had a wireless set because they would be the ones who could afford to give him a meal.

One day another woman saw him come round the side of her house towards the door, and remarked to her husband: "Oh look, here's this old beggar coming again." Larry heard her say this, and when she opened the door he gave her a proper talking-to for calling him an old beggar.

"I'm no old beggar," he insisted. "I'm a legitimate traveller."

Of course, some people did give him a welcome. "Why, it's Mr Sinclair—come inside," was the way one housewife always greeted him. Another man said he liked to see Larry turn up so as to get all the local news, and no doubt Larry felt everyone should give him this kind of welcome.

Sometimes he would take offence where none was intended. At one farm he was allowed to sleep in a hut, and finding a supply of firewood handy, he lit the fire. But it was springtime, starlings had begun building their nests in the chimney . . . Suddenly the door burst open and Larry emerged with his swag on his back followed by a great cloud of smoke, and without stopping he hurried on in a huff to the next farm to seek a night's lodging, presumably blaming the people he had just walked out on for blocking the chimney deliberately.

On another visit at the same farm, Larry was taken into the house for a meal. Handed a cup of tea, he immediately 'saucered' it. Just as he was raising the saucer to his mouth to take a sip, he suddenly sneezed, blowing a veritable shower of tea across the table and straight into the face of the lady of the house, whose expression of horror and disgust had to be seen to be believed.

Some say he used to take on an occasional job during the turnip thinning season, but this is the only mention I have ever heard of him working. An uncle of mine at Mataura once told him:

"I'm sick of feeding you for nothing, Dave Sinclair. If

you want work, I'll give you work, but you needn't expect to come here and get free meals."

Larry, deeply offended of course, picked up his swag and stalked off to the next door neighbours, complaining that the east wind had put my uncle in bad humour.

As far as my own personal recollections of old Larry are concerned, I can remember him calling at my home sometime in the early 1930s. I was not very old at the time but I remember a bushy grey beard, and I seem to picture him walking with a forward lean, but of course this is understandable when he had spent most of his life carrying a swag.

However, I can still see him accepting a mug of tea outside the back door. My mother had just finished clearing up after dinner, and it did not suit her just then to ask Larry inside. Of course this would be a crime in Larry's eyes. He would think he had the right to be asked into every home he visited. At any rate, after this he didn't call on us again for a good number of years.

When he did call at my home again, one night in September 1944, my parents were both milking the cows. Meeting my mother first as he entered the byre he demanded:

"Where's the boss?"

Mother directed him down to the other end of the shed where he asked my father if he could be put up for the night?

"Right," replied dad, "you can make yourself a shakedown in the chaff barn."

"What about some tea?"

"We'll send some out to you at the barn when we've finished milking."

Larry paced up and down between the byre and the barn, muttering to himself.

Milking finished, mother went straight to the house but she hadn't even time to wash before Larry was at the door demanding his tea.

"I haven't had time to get it ready yet," mum tells him.

"It takes you a mighty long time to milk a few cows."

"None of your impudence," says mum, "get away back to the barn and we'll send you something when it's ready."

Larry went off in a very bad humour. We sent him out a tray with a mug of tea and a few meat and cheese sandwiches.

Next morning, when mum sent dad to collect Larry's tray in order to send him out some breakfast, he returned with the tray and the news "Your bird's flown." Larry had disappeared. Mind you, it was spring, the young calves were housed in the loosebox just through the wall from where Larry was sleeping, and their spirited chorus would wake Larry at an early hour. Incidentally, when the tray was returned, the sandwiches had been opened, the meat and cheese eaten, but the bread and butter left.

About 8.15 that morning on my way to catch the train to school, I saw Larry pacing the main street of Edendale by the Post Office.

Soon after 9.00 a.m. that same morning my uncle, William Hall, who had seen the swagger at our place the day before, went into the Post Office and here was Larry collecting his old age pension.

"Look here, Sinclair," says Uncle Bill, "you shouldn't be drawing a pension and going round living on the farmers at the same time."

"I'll need it all after the treatment I got down there last night," growled Larry.

Six months later, about 10 o'clock one morning, my mother opened the door to a knock. Larry stood there. He seemed rather taken aback. Perhaps his memory by this time was failing and he had forgotten that here on his last visit he hadn't been treated exactly as an honoured guest.

"Wh-what's the time?" he stammers, "I was wondering if I could get a cup of tea?"

"The kettle's not boiling," replies mum, "but I suppose you could have a cup of tea if you like to wait for it. But remember, you weren't very polite last time you were here."

"Don't want to hear about that," retorts Larry.

"Maybe not," says mum, "but you're just as well to be reminded of it."

Larry turned and walked off without waiting for his tea. That was the last time we saw him.

Around this time he began going into the Riverton Old Men's Home for the winters, but he didn't like it there because his pension was taken from him and he was allowed only a few shillings a week for pocket money. So when summer came, he would take to the roads again. Time, though, forced him to become a permanent inmate, and there he died some 25 years ago.

'The Fattening Paddock'

The Fattening Paddock stretched for swaggers from Kaikoura to Flaxbourne—dusty, bronzed, distinctive, proud Marlborough, a province of great variation and contrast in so many ways, has its own swagger stories with some intangible, indefinable touch evolving, and with my thanks to collector Joy Shepard of Yelverton, we have a Marlborough chapter opening with this brisk sample:

'Monkey' Sharp enjoyed playing the piano, and very well too, at the old Waihopai Hotel, Wairau Valley, his speciality and favourite *The Bluebells of Scotland* with elaborate variations. This time, he was giving trills and runs with great force, in fact with such force that he fouled his pants.

Years later, when Jean (of the hotel family) was a schoolgirl learning to play the piano, her mum would say:

"You're all right, but you can't play the piano with variations like Billy Sharp."

And Jean would reply: "I wouldn't want to."

'Monkey' (Bill) Sharp, once a bank teller and the brother of a strongly-disapproving lawyer; a well-educated, tidily-dressed, shy and quietly spoken man seldom seeking the company of the station hands, a drinker never in trouble with the law. His regular beat, lasting several months and providing him with food and secondhand clothes, took him through the sheep stations of Wairau Valley, the Waihopai and the Awatere—three days with the Watsons at Renwick; on three miles to the evening meal of fried chops, potatoes, and rice pudding and a good bed in the men's quarters at William Pollard's The Delta; chops, bread, and a great pannikin of embalming-fluid tea for breakfast, then two miles on to Valleyfield where the cook would quarry two huge meat sandwiches to take to a snug sheltered spot on the Omaka River bed, an ideal place to pass the day reading . . .

Tall, lean, lazy, his was "a small face with a wide mouth, and the particular way he screwed up his face somewhat when talking gave a monkey-look."

Matriculating at Nelson College (1867-74), he joined the Bank of New South Wales, hence his habit of changing any cash smartly into sixpences. With beer sixpence a glass, he never bought more than one drink at a time.

His billy was a big jam tin, black as the ace of spades, and Ernie Ball, waggoner between Hillersden and Blenheim and often giving him a lift, was invited by Monkey to join him in a drink of tea, but "strange to say I wasn't thirsty."

A very small boy Jim Corrigan, today a veteran journalist at Pahiatua, had long conversations with him while Jim's mother prepared food for the swagger: "One such conversation took place after I had just started school.

"In his perfect diction he asked: 'And how do you like school? Can you read yet?'

"My reply was that I did not want to read.

" 'Tut! Tut! my boy,' he exclaimed in mock horror. 'If you don't learn to read, you will never be able to read our beautiful English language. You must learn to read, and next time I come round I'll expect you to read me a story.'

"I am not sure about the result, but I think I did read him a short story from one of the Primer books of those days."

"Bill Sharp was grateful to Dick Seddon—whose government made provision for the submerged tenth of our people," writes Herbert Watson of Renwick.

"We missed the old man of the road when old age caught up with him and those old legs let him down. But he found a good friend in Archie Adams of Langley Dale Station near Renwick, a community warm with hospitality." (Once told at Langley Dale they didn't have any meat, Bill went off saying he'd have to have a look at the meat safe, peered through, came back, and said reproachfully: "You have so.")

Bill was given a comfortable whare at Rock Ferry with

plenty of firewood for the gathering, and close to the road with little walking needed to pick up his stores.

"This neatly dressed old tramp became too frail, the grocer serving him each week found him very ill, and took him to the Wairau Hospital where he died in peace and comfort in the 1940s.

"Quiet and inoffensive, he was the last of his kind, and we missed him very much as a reminder of the scores who once passed through our beloved township of Renwick."

Mrs Bob Wallace of Blenheim remembers many swaggers had no socks and she would give them a bowl of water to bathe their feet. They'd cut a hedge or chop wood, have a bowl of soup, accept her packet of sandwiches and a billy of tea, then off again.

Many a youngster beamed when a swagger came into the backyard—no more wood to chop for a day or two! Yet (as many anticipated) it was simple for a caller to break an axehandle 'purely by accident', and others discouraged chopping in case they might be saddled with an injured swagger for a week or more.

Always first asking for an axe on arrival and striding off to cut a pile of wood before seeking a meal from the Douglas family at Flaxmere, 'Velveteen Jack', never without his velveteen jacket, provided the stovewood for dozens of Marlborough ranges.

At Rockwood, near Kaikoura, a huge open woodshed backed onto the back door. It was always kept full of sawn-up wood, an obvious sight to the swaggers calling. If they didn't really want a job, they'd say to Mrs George Dublin Smith:

"Could we cut wood for you missus?"—knowing full well the woodshed was chocker.

The late Lex Mowat, born at Altimarloch recounted this story to Tom Maddever, the present owner of the station.

Fed and bedded down for the night at Altimarloch, with the customary expectation he'd cut up a bit of wood, a swagger departed early next morning leaving this note.

'I saw the saw but never saw the saw saw.'

'The Fattening Paddock'

On the Marlborough-Nelson border, near the old Bulford bridge, there by the Rai River and bush, stood a hut with a generous bed of dry ferns on the floor, a good stop for the night because folk round about would leave supplies in the hut such as potatoes, onions, a bit of flour or dripping, a screw of salt, maybe a little treacle or sugar for the man on that trail.

At Blind River, Seddon, Mollie Casey's mother was about to stoke up the fuel range to cook some eggs for this swagger, but he exclaimed: "No, don't do that—no trouble—they'll be fine as they are, thanks," and down the lane he strolled, sucking the raw eggs with obvious relish.

Some were not pleased with a handout of bread and jam—said it was only fit for children—but women with large families could find difficulty in providing extra meals because so often money was scarce.

Two delicious soles, done to a turn, and Rosina Corlett and her mother were on the very point of sitting down to a special breakfast in the farmhouse near Blenheim in 1925, when a swagger nearly sixty appeared. One sole generously was given to the old chap to eat outside, while mother and daughter shared the remaining fish.

When they went out later, he had finished his meal but they saw with eyes growing wider and wider that he had eaten only the centre out of both sides, *leaving the rest!*

To see her 'lost sole' treated like this was too much—and when he said it was his third breakfast that morning, daughter saw red, told him off, and exclaimed if he dared to poke his nose back there or tell any of his cobbers to call, she would 'sool' them down the road with the dog. He, or his mates, never appeared again.

Round the Wairau Valley, at Mt Patriarch, Sybil Lupp was working with the family in the field when three ravenous swaggers turned up and were told to go ahead up to the house and into the kitchen and to help themselves to bread, butter, and a pot of stew simmering on the stove (records Anthony James).

"But just make sure you leave enough for us."

An hour later, the three returned, beaming and deeply

appreciative. To show their thanks, they took the hoes from the workers and began energetically hoeing the potatoes.

"When the family went home, the stew was untouched, but the swaggers in error had eaten a great pot of bones and rejects we'd boiled up for the dogs."

You can't help wondering maybe that was a repast "just like mother used to make?"

One swagger would camp in an empty house handy to Blenheim, nip neighbours for something to eat, then on Saturdays go to town in more ways than one. On Sundays he would be going up and down the road singing out: "Hee Haw, Hee Haw," somewhat like a bleary donkey.

Another sorely-troubled man years ago was the chemist at Havelock, not really a swagger but a sudden and impetuous refugee on the roads, calling on the pretext of buying calves, always sick in appearance, rocking on his heels, needing brandy or whisky. Marlburians would keep him for a day or so then send him back to Havelock when he'd sobered up.

He was at his worst when he'd been swigging the bottles of scent from his stock! That gave him the DTs. To get him right, Constable Douglas would send him out to "a kindly, capable countrywoman with a wish to help the sick and needy."

She held a firm belief in the popular bottled 'cure-all' mixture then called Painkiller, but her son decided to mix up his own Painkiller brew—into this prescription for the suffering chemist went cayenne pepper, ginger, honey, vinegar, Worcestershire sauce, mustard—all things hot and beautiful in measures great and small, plus a dash of milk. The chemist "downed it like a lamb" and asked for more, saying it did him a power of good. After that, he was even more reluctant to return to Havelock.

"When the skin was cracking," as they put it, they just had to head for a drink. When Frank Parker from the Clarence River (we are indebted to him for our chapter title 'The Fattening Paddock') came into Blenheim one day he found a big argument in progress on the footpath in front of the old Post Office. The policeman was arresting Charlie Hodson, who'd just ended a bit of work for the Parkers, for being under the influence—Charlie's swag was lying on the footpath, he flatly refusing to pick it up, maintaining emphatically that if they wanted to put him in jail, *they* could carry it!

A little old disgruntled man pushing a pram holding all his possessions stayed briefly at Altimarloch, sharpened scissors and charged for this, also for some gardening. He kept asking for milk which he must have laced, for Peggy Maddever looked out to see him (as she sees him yet) haphazardly prodding the soil with a fork and "scratching along the garden like an old chook." Despite his free bed and tucker while there, with payment for work done, when the time came for him to leave Tom Maddever took him down the road but got a surprise to be told, "You owe me for a loaf." (Earlier he had handed over a stale half-loaf.)

Much more professional was Tom Bray, putting bright touches to many Marlborough gardens and even working in Hales Nursery for a while until the urge came to head south to Christchurch, Arthur's Pass, and back up Marlborough way again, once even crossing to the North Island to garden for a while at Beetham's in the Wairarapa.

Just on dark a swagger with a mad look in his eyes made Blairich to tell Con Newman he'd been bitten by a katipo—as he came up the East Coast. Con took him to the old whare and started up the boiler, for the swagman did have a bit of a swelling, but either the terrible groans and explosions from the ancient boiler, or the prospect of washing so alarmed the patient that he left in a cloud of dust.

Blairich, Upton Downs, and Welds Hill were taken over by the Bank towards the end of last century (when most big sheep stations were in trouble financially) and a Mr Young was appointed manager. He would stop one night or longer at each place, for they were only four or five miles apart. A. West, of the Awatere Valley was told by an eye-witness shepherd:

At Blairich, Mr Young saw two swaggers arrive to stop

the night, one white one black. Next night at Upton Downs he spotted the couple arriving there, and the following night, beheld them turning up at Welds Hill!

Noticing him for the first time, they asked permission for a shakedown.

"Certainly," said Mr Young, adding as a joke, "How far have you come from today?"

"Oh, from Dumgree—about 20 miles away."

"Strange, strange indeed, because I saw you at Blairich two nights back, at Upton Downs last night, and you're here tonight!"

This was too much for the white man—he wouldn't stop. The black fellow still insisted they'd come from Dumgree that day.

Next morning a shepherd said to the black chap: "By Jove the boss caught you out last night, eh?"

"I know he did," replied the dark one, *"but when you tell a lie you have to stick to it."*

Coming away from the inland hills and down towards the coast for a while, the Goulter farm, Starborough, was right by the township of Seddon, on the main south road, near the Awatere road-rail bridge. Miss K. E. Goulter now takes up the tale:

Over this bridge all north or south bound traffic flowed, and during the depression a procession of out of work men passed right at our back door. And many stopped there.

How many?

During the first six months of 1932, my father gave out 206 chits, good for a meal at Mrs Walker's boardinghouse, but as the depression closed down on the farmers, money became tight, and the meagre working budget the Bank permitted my father, forced him to close his swaggers-account at Mrs Walker's. From then on the 'men off the road' were fed by my mother with a handout at the door.

'Men off the road' . . .

During my childhood, the depression years, I never heard my parents refer to 'tramps' or 'swaggers', always 'a man off the road'. How many times have I heard my mother call one of us children to go to the old bakery and get a stale sandwich loaf because there was 'a man off the road'? And the taciturn, old Scots baker would silently pull back the clean white sack which covered what was left of yesterday's bach, and hand out the loaf. No money was passed. We had an account, but I don't think he ever charged for these so-called 'stale' loaves, and very often they were of the day's batch.

The men off the road rarely asked directly for food. They merely presented their blackened billies at the kitchen door with the invariable: "Could you spare us a drink of tea, Missus?" And while the big iron kettle on the range came to the boil, my mother would make up the handout—several enormously thick sandwiches, the bread thickly buttered with our own separator butter, and filled with chunks of cold mutton, all wrapped in the previous day's *Marlborough Express*—we found the men appreciated this reading matter as much as anything.

On nights when two, maybe three, were waiting at the back door for sandwiches, the family tea would be boiled eggs only. A leg or a shoulder of mutton will only stretch so far . . . and these men were hungry. If my father had not killed that week, and consequently there was no cold mutton, my mother hard-boiled several eggs and the men got these, with bread and butter, not forgetting salt in a screw of paper. Sometimes mother added a slice or two of Victorian sandwich and old-fashioned, madeira type cake, baked in a large meat dish, split open while hot and filled with homemade jam.

What were those men like? A child is not very observant, but I remember one thing: *their stillness.*

They rarely smiled, and seldom spoke, except to thank for the handout, and to add the invariable "Any chance of a shakedown for the night?" They were directed to the whare—the shearers' quarters, empty most of the year—and there were mattresses, blankets, and a good fire, for anyone who picked up the wood from the nearby plantation. It was open house. How many slept there? No one will ever know. My father kept no record, but over the depression years the tally must have run into many hundreds.

Drink? Very little among 'the men off the road'. Unemployment, not alcohol, was their problem.

I have heard of children being frightened of 'tramps', but we never were. The men who came to our backdoor were just "those poor men" and our parents taught us to meet them with the same respect and good manners as any visitor to our home.

One who came several times, a returned soldier, was a pitiful wreck of a man, shaking with what they called 'shell shock' in those days. We called him 'Fairy' because my little sister was dressed as a fairy, waiting to go to a fancy dress party, the first time he came, and he was entranced. He always asked to see his 'little fairy' every time he came.

He gave her a piece of watered silk ribbon and told her that it was very precious. She thought it just a pretty piece of ribbon. Later we realised that it was cut from his Anzac service medal. Poor 'Fairy', he had so little to give and *that* was the most valued thing he possessed. After that we never saw him again.

Affection still lingers like a faintly thinning mist in a few elderly minds round Seddon for Tom Riley who came to Galtymore each year, medium height, cleanshaven except for a moustache, a very clean and particular man, carried a fairly big swag with billy, and always walked—a real 'professional swaggie'. Tom smoked a pipe for which he had made a little tin cap with holes in it and always put that over the top.

Every harvest for over ten years he'd be calling at Galtymore and he would see the job through, always pleased and excited to get back. When younger he would fork in the paddock. Bill Maher took photos of him around 1930 stooking, and one of him in the dray with his favourite horse Madam, an old dark grey mare he idolised. She was so quiet and easy to handle. The Maher boys, when they got the chance, gave Madam a poke in the rump with a stick just to make her jump and worry Tom. One morning at breakfast they told him that Madam was lame. Tom never said a word, just got up from the table, left his meal, went over to the shed and let her out, afterwards telling them "You shouldn't have said that—I might have left."

Tom used to scare the kids by telling them that often when the stacks were burnt, they'd find the bones of the 'straw-wallopers' who had been covered over by accident when stacking. The kids almost believed it. Airguns were great fun and one day Jim Maher was encouraged by Tom to stalk and shoot at a bird on a fence. Jim got so near that he thought he just couldn't miss but his careful stalking was a flop as Tom had the bird 'tied' to the fence.

The Maher boys used to go down to the train to pick up an old character who worked for them, Peter Roberts. He always brought back a crate of beer with him. This time he'd been back on the farm two days and Tom Riley was slinging off at the old chap just to annoy him, saying "Have you seen the second gardener?" (meaning Peter) as though *he* was the first. One morning about 5.30, Bill Maher got up and found Tom walking round dressed up, quite disturbed as Peter had come home the night before and was still very much under the weather. He was worried about it because Peter was "walking round in his shirt-tail with legs like sticks" and Tom thought he might do him in.

For a time he seemed to disappear. The last time he came back he just walked round for two days, talking to them, so happy to be back. Bill saw him then as a real old man about sixty, difficult to place as the joyous lithe companion of the harvest days, always playing tricks and making cricket bats out of willow for the Maher family's Sunday cricket matches.

> *Swagging is an Honest Trade*
> *Which wealthy Knaves Despise*
> *Yet Rich Folks may be Swaggers made*
> *And we who swag may Rise.*

Charlie Stuart of Marlborough Sounds, our poet just quoted (with apologies to Robbie Burns) met swaggers at a big sheep and cattle station in Marlborough in 1930, carrying their possessions mostly in a sugarbag strapped to their back.

The old swagger, others have observed, usually carried his swag straight up and down his back; the new chum his swag swung across his back, billy hanging from the end.

Yarning away, his liking for them increasing the more he heard and learned, "they looked on life with a challenge and met it with a smile, and always prepared to tackle life as it lay ahead, living today as well they may, regardless of tomorrow. It was a challenge that they never lost, with the attitude that there is no armour against fate, and that men had been knighted for less deeds than being an 'Honest Swagger'.

"They certainly knew their way around and gained knowledge in their own environment on surviving through difficult weather and obtaining food and shelter, which no doubt are the main necessities in life."

One character, after travelling the North Island, by shrewdness and skill talked his way from Wellington to Picton on the ferry at no expense, with a free feed chucked into the bargain. He arrived at the station cowshed during the afternoon milking, and after a good fill of fresh warm milk, asked Charlie:

"Would the boss allow me a feed and a lie down for the night?"

"Oh I'm sure he would—I can't think of anyone just now who've been refused. No. You'll be right if you ask the boss at the homestead."

He did, had a meal, went off to a hut, and almost at once fell fast asleep, with loud snores discouraging a visit. He called at the cookhouse next morning, for a good solid breakfast, and Charlie from the cowshed, watched him pass on down the road . . .

That afternoon another swagger appeared, opened the gate to the homestead with assurance, soon reappeared at the cookhouse, had a feed, and went to the hut.

Strolling over for a yarn and crossing the doorway, Charlie soon stepped back for a breather, recoiling from a cloud of strong smoke.

"What on earth brand of tobacco are you smoking?"

'The Fattening Paddock' 75

"No tobacco. Only dried gumleaves and dockleaves to keep the bally mosquitoes away from me in the night."

After talking for a while:

"Aren't you the chap who called at the cowshed last night?"

He hesitated for a moment, then said:

"Er—how did you know?"

"By your voice. But . . . didn't you have a beard?"

After a good laugh, he replied with an endearing grin:

"You see, us swaggers have got to use our heads to get through this world. Yesterday morning when I left, I headed up the road for a few miles and learned that us blokes aren't too welcome, as the farms are only small. So I retreated, had a sleep in the shade, then cut off my beard with a pair of scissors. Then I put on another hat, came back to the homestead, and asked the boss for the essential favour.

"He said: 'Go up and see the cook and get on your way in the morning—and—wait a bit—haven't I seen you here sometime before?'

" 'Yes,' I said, 'almost a year today.' "

The boss nodded, silently congratulating himself on a not-too-bad memory.

That night, Charlie Stuart was silently ruminating: if this traveller of the highways and byways had no ambition, he certainly made up for it with skill.

For two seasons, in 1922-3, Lew Timms at 19 was the youngest of 13 musterers at Molesworth Station. Bred and born for the job, he was a descendant of a pioneer family arriving from Leeds, Staffordshire, in the 1840s to farm one side of the Upper Clarence Valley, then buying Northbank Station on the Wairau River. He remembers the venerated George Clark of Port Levy, near Lyttelton, who rode his horse all the way from there via Jollies Pass to Molesworth, to become a musterer on the station—riding the route taken by many of the hardy swaggers on the back trails.

Before Lew bought his first farm in the Wairau Valley in 1925, he started a memorable taxi service there in 1923 with a Model T Ford, and drove to and from Blenheim, his passengers including one Christmas Eve, his wife-to-be, who was working on Lansdowne Station. One dusty trudger in particular in their minds is Tom Long, called 'The Hangman'. He really had the valley kids scared because they'd been told with a gruesome flourish or two that he was the hangman in Blenheim.

Through the Wairau regularly in about 1930 came a traveller thought to be named Murphy, swagging on horseback, his dog padding alongside him.

"Just a billy of hot water thanks, that's all I want," Murphy told a valley housewife.

As she took his billy and went to the stove to fill it, she lifted the lid—and there to her amazement nestled a live pup only about two days old! Probably his dog had pups on the trail, Murphy thought he'd save one, and had briefly forgotten he'd popped it into the billy for the ride.

Another swagger entered the Waihopai Valley seeking a bit of stovewood to cut, but Mr Cresswell the farmer said he'd potatoes to dig and took the swagger out to the paddock to see them. The old rover surveyed the long rows with increasing gloom, shook his head dubiously, and grumbled firmly:

"I dunno, I don't think I'll dig 'em, as I might stick a fork through 'em all . . ."

Before the First World War many swaggers, mostly in pairs, walked the Blenheim-Nelson road (writes L. C. Leov from Havelock). "Judge our surprise when I was at school around 1904 when a swagger turned up humping a small organ with a monkey on top for a swag! He called at the old Flat Creek school, Rai Valley, just before morning lessons began, and gave a great demonstration of what he and the monkey could do. He turned a handle to get a tune and the monkey set to work, jumping from the organ onto the man's head, leaping into the air, turning somersaults, and landing in some funny positions, all to the tune from the organ. He amused us for a good half hour, then our teacher, Miss McMahon, went to her house, got a few shillings, and gave them to the monkey. I must say the pair had provided an amusement we 25 or so kids could never forget.

"All tramps were not useless. Two young chaps called at

my sister's place, Rai Valley. They'd walked all the way from Timaru and wanted a feed. She was just going to do the evening milking. Her husband was away. The two young chaps bogged in and helped with the cows. She was so pleased with them and their efforts that she phoned several friends and got jobs for them on two different farms. They eventually married local girls and were good citizens."

One swagger, Halliday, still quietly admired by Ernie Ball, now a retired farmer, was lame in one leg, couldn't work on the dray or stack, but helped at harvest time. With his fork—when no 'crow' was used—he could toss the sheaves "high and mighty, right up and over" from the ground to Ernie sweating away who'd work them into place on the stack.

But his most poignant memory of them all is of the tall active man in middleage carrying a swag and asking for a job—to Ernie a swaggie asking for a job was usually treated as a joke. However, to his surprise "he turned out to be the best teamster, or one of the best, I ever had, he took the horses off the grass and in a little while had a goodlooking team. He was a quiet chap, did his work, minded his own business, and we got on well; in those days a farmer worked hard, and all he thought about after his day's work was bed.

"He was with us some months until one day something must have upset him, we never found out what it was. Anyway about all he would say for days was 'yes' or 'no'. I didn't like it: after all we were over a mile from our nearest neighbour: I had my wife and the kiddies to think of. But this blew over until some months later the same thing happened.

"This time I made up my mind he would have to go. I gave him notice.

"He took it quite meekly, he had a fair cheque coming to him as he had drawn only tobacco money all the time he was with us, and he asked me a favour: would I mind taking him to the train at Auripo, 'Because,' he said, 'if I get in the pub at Ida Valley, my cheque will be cut out and that's as far as I'll get on my journey.'

"I have his name in my old wage book, I feel he had come from very decent people, also I think he was a returned soldier, probably the booze was his trouble. We were sorry to see him go; looking back now one thinks surely this could have been handled differently."

Back north for our final Marlborough story from Herbert Watson of Renwick:
I was cooking my tea at my bach in the Rai in the winter of 1927 when an old man came to my door. Might he be allowed to put his horse in my back paddock for the night? Of course.

I showed him where his horse could be safely paddocked, and invited him to join me at the teatime meal. I noticed that he and his horse were inseparable friends, the animal becoming upset when he was out of sight for any length of time.

When he came in for his meal I shut the door to keep in the warmth for the air was cold and frosty, but his pal tore up and down the fenceline whinneying away in great distress. The old man, full of apologies for the turmoil, asked if he could sit at the end of the table to allow the horse to see him through the open door.

As soon as this was done, the horse stood with his head over the fence, in full view of his human 'brother'—there is scarcely another way, or word, to convey this strong affectionate relationship.

Tea over, what a relief for me to draw close to the roaring matai fire in the dover stove.

"Now supper will be ready at 9 o'clock," I told my visitor, but when the time came and no guest was around I began a search in the outbuildings, in the hay pile, and then, puzzled, along the row of pine trees.

Abruptly, the stamp of the horse's feet began on the other side of the fence. As I approached, he gave a short whinney to warn his sleeping mate danger was around.

There lay the old chap, covered with white frost, on a bed of pine needles. His only covering was a single dark blanket and an ancient overcoat.

I explained supper was waiting, with a warm fire roaring away. He protested that sleeping under the stars was common to him and gave him no discomfort. His horse expected him to be always close at hand and got very upset when he lost sight of him.

"Heavens no!" I told him back. "I just couldn't possibly sleep in a soft cosy bed while you shivered out here in a frosty hard bed."

After a long harangue he came inside, we sat over a delayed supper, and when the horse's racket subsided and the hot tea warmed his body, he went to bed in his clothes.

Next morning he was up bright and early to bridle and saddle his horse before breakfast. He accepted a packet of meat sandwiches and placed it in his saddlebag.

"Is a police officer stationed at Havelock?"

Curious, I wondered: was he in trouble with the law? No, he explained, but a police officer had picked him up for vagrancy, and he could pass through the town only during the hours of darkness through dark streets.

His hardships rather saddened and depressed me.

"Why not settle in some empty whare during the winter months and live in more congenial conditions?"

Oh no, not at all, this was not for him. He and his horse, which he never rode, were close friends who loved a roving life close to nature. "Oh no, I couldn't settle down. I just *have* to wander." Work had no interest. It tied one down to boredom and monotony.

I thoroughly enjoyed the old chap and his devoted horse. They were a loyal pair, who lived and loved each other so intensely.

On 25 June, 1976, three friends found in Omaka Cemetery a small white broken stone reading 'William Lawson Sharp born 1855 died 1942 aged 86 years': 'Monkey', ex-bank teller, in pauper's ground, the stone from his only mourner, farmer Archie Adams.

Grandmother's Extraordinary Confinement

An old swagger used to stop over at the station on his way back from the West Coast—he was usually recovering from a bout or 'trip' on meths—and while 'convalescing' did a few odd jobs, cutting firewood, a bit of fencing and so on. After he'd dried out, Grandad usually gave him a plug or two of tobacco for his pipe, a few dry rations, and a couple of pairs of hand-knitted sox (well darned), and perhaps a warm old jacket. Then the old swagger would saunter off, either back to the Coast, or towards Springfield if he could get a lift across the river on a wagon. But he never told anyone of his plans, and he'd turn up at the homestead maybe twice a year.

Now Grandma had had a genteel upbringing in Scotland and was hardly suited to the rugged life in early New Zealand's backblocks, on this sheep station in the foothills of the Southern Alps in the mid-1800s.

Nevertheless (wrote D. A. Goss to me from Havelock North), she had thirteen babies over the years, and I think ten of them survived. My mother was the eldest. As time for

Grandmother's Extraordinary Confinement 81

the birth of the second baby drew near, Grandad and one of the station shepherds set off with a wagon to Springfield, to bring back the old Maori midwife and collect stores. Besides Grandma and the first child (who was just a toddler) and a few shepherds, the only people on the place were the Chinese station cook, Hing, and this swagger, deep in an alcoholic daze.

Grandad and the midwife were due back from Springfield but they struck real trouble. The bridge over the Kowhai River had been washed away. The fords over the Waimak and Kowhai, due to snow on the Alps melting early and flooding the rivers, were not fordable. So the wagon was held up between the two rivers.

Picture the perturbation when Hing the Chinese cook came over to the homestead early one morning to get flour and odds and ends for the cookhouse and found Grandma in early labour.

The shepherds had left the night before to go into the foothills for an early muster—poor old Hing was certainly on the spot! As luck would have it, the old meths swagger, on one of his visits, was drying out in an old hut near the riverbed. Hing got him on his feet, made him a "welly stlong blew of black tea" and told him the story.

Hing panicked and was, I suppose, all for getting the old opium pipe out, but the swagger chap took command—only after Hing had made him shed his old clothes, and stood him outside in a tub and really got to work on him with hot water, scrubbing brush and sheep dip (which was a bit strong)—Jeyes fluid solution.

Grannie nearly died of fright when she saw her medical team—a pigtailed Chinaman shivering with fright and an apparition gowned in one of Grandad's long night shirts, a pillowcase tied over his head and a pair of Chinese slippers on his feet—but by this time she needed help badly.

Strange to say, the swagger chap seemed to know his job. By this time he was giving the orders, and Hing was jumping to it.

The baby was at last delivered and washed and bedded down in the old wooden crib. Grannie was amazed when her "midwife chap" tore off a piece of white linen, scorched it over the stove fire, and tied the umbilical cord in a very professional manner indeed.

When Grandad returned, the new baby, a boy, was two days old. Grannie, quite comfortable, fed on everyday cookhouse tucker, her nurse fussing over the place and his patient with full authority. It transpired the old swagger was a remittance man from England, had been a medical student for three years in London, came from a medical family, but became an alcoholic, could not pass his degree exams, and was sent out to the 'colonies' in disgrace. He spent his remittance from home on any liquor he could buy, then took to the road again until the next cheque from England arrived.

Grannie said that for ever after that, Hing showed not the usual contempt for the swagger chap, but referred to him as '*Mr* Doctor', even allowed him to have the odd meal in the cookhouse, and always gave him supper at night. Hitherto, he'd referred to him as 'he' or 'him' and gave him a meal on the chopping block or door step.

Now Grandad was a very strict Presbyterian gentleman, and after breakfast on Sunday mornings all the family and station hands gathered in the homestead dining room for prayers and a reading from the bible. On the first Sunday after the birth of the baby, (the first son in the family), all were assembled as usual and by special invitation, 'Mr Doctor'!

Grandad gave thanks to God for the safe delivery of the baby. Next, he invited the special guest to read a chapter from the bible. This he did in a very well-educated, indeed cultured tone of voice, pronouncing without hesitation all the difficult names and passages to the amazement of the station hands present, who had always thought of him merely as 'the swagger bloke from the Coast'.

For years after that, when he arrived at the homestead and again when he left, he was always asked to partake of a drachm of Grandad's Scotch whisky as an honoured guest of the station. Though Grandad never gave his reasons why, he insisted on his first son being called Henry, and the baby was duly christened 'Henry Robert MacKay'. Everyone

Grandmother's Extraordinary Confinement 83

suspected that the swagger's name was Henry 'someone' and Grandad honoured him by naming the first of the many sons he had, after the tramp from the Coast. My Uncle Henry lived to a great old age, and was loved by all of us.

My mother told us that old Hing the cook, with his pigtail, for many years smoked his opium pipe and made the best station bread ever. As Henry the 'swagger bloke' had not been seen on the station for some time, Grandad made inquiries, and found he'd drowned while trying to cross the Waimakariri River.

Lonely and unloved lives, cadging a meal and a bed from place to place, sometimes burned to death in a hut, or to die in their sleep from an overdose of meths. Whether humble, or work-shy, or booted out in disgrace from some high-ranking English family, may they all rest in peace, which life seemed to deny them.

One of our house cows was due to calve and dad went up the hill to see if she was all right. He came back very agitated, told me to saddle my pony, go across to our neighbour and ask him to bring a pack horse: "And hurry!" My eyes were popping when later, dad and the neighbour Reg, came very slowly down the hill with the person I knew only as Old Fred the Swagger draped across the pack horse. He'd passed through our property several times before, receiving handouts at the back door.

Mother took charge from then on. She'd made up a bed in what we used to call the verandah room, and the men got the patient stripped of his wet soiled clothes, and washed and rubbed warm and clad in a pair of dad's pyjamas. He looked lost in them. Dad was 6'5" tall and a big chap. Poor old Fred was skinny and wizened and shrunken.

He raised his first smiles when mother put a clean folded snowy white handkerchief in the pyjama pocket—he caressed it rather sadly.

He must have been in a bad way when he was found asleep in the cow byre: no food, wet to the skin, and the nights then were frosty. However, a tot of father's Scotch and some bowls of good soup and he began to look less blue and more human—he probably had pneumonia.

At the time, I was having music lessons (piano) from a German music teacher who came through the district about once a month. He had bushy eyebrows and a Kaiser William moustache and was bossy and very formidable. I was terrified of him. He used to rap my knuckles quite hard with a thick blue pencil. I loved music. I still do, and eventually did very well with piano playing.

Soon, old Fred was well enough to get up for a few hours and walk up and down the verandah.

I was in the dining room practising exercises and scales. Mum had come out to give Fred his morning broth and medicine and he asked her permission to correct my piano exercise, as I was not playing it right—he sat on the stool and showed me how it should be played and didn't rap my knuckles.

Then he played one of my pieces, and from then on I loved him dearly.

Every day he helped me with my music and I was quite pleased when I heard that Herman the German had fallen off his horse and broken his leg and would not return. My father, Welsh and Irish, 50/50, of course was a music lover. He had a glorious bass baritone voice, and was in great demand locally for concerts and social events. Old Fred played *Larboard Watch, Asleep in the Deep* etc, and dad sang and we had some great musical evenings at our place.

Fred looked very distinguished from the neck up, prematurely grey hair and lively eyes, but he didn't look all that hot below the neck as he still wore father's O.S. clothes, and Fred was very small and still thin. However, dad outfitted him when an itinerant draper passed through the district, mum knitted him a cardigan, and he looked quite sporty in tweedy jacket, waistcoat, pants, and a bow tie.

My father was choirmaster at our local Church of England and he began taking old Fred to choir practice. Archbishop Julius was to administer confirmation in the parish and the choir began to practise furiously—even aimed at an anthem.

Fred play the organ, and the choir rose to his music and

Grandmother's Extraordinary Confinement

sang as they had never done before. Mother 'made down' and starched a spare surplice and old Fred, with his grey hair and bow tie, looked just great on the day and was complimented by the archbishop on his beautiful music.

I remember Fred taking us all out on the verandah one starry night and showing me Halley's Comet in the sky. He explained what it was and told me that the next time the comet appeared in the sky over New Zealand he, Fred, would be playing a harp in Heaven and I'd be rocking my grandchildren on my knee.

At that time the New Zealand census of population was being taken and dad had to ask Fred, who still lived under our roof, what his surname was. He told dad it was Harrow.

He was well enough by now to move on. My father started him off on piano tuning jobs through the district and he did quite well at this. I missed his pianoforte lessons but I practised like mad so he would be pleased with me when he came back.

Time passed. He didn't return.

When he had been missing for some months, father went to Christchurch, made a few inquiries, and found poor old Fred in a Salvation Army Home for Men—very depressed and penniless, and in the process of drying out from a whisky drinking bout. Whisky was his weakness, yet all the time he was with us after his illness, after the first good nip dad gave him to thaw out, he always refused a drink of whisky when it was offered, and there would always be an opened bottle of Johnny Walker in the sideboard cupboard in the dining room, yet he never once accepted a drop.

His family in England thought he must have died out in New Zealand as the remittances of money had been returned to them, unclaimed, so father wrote to the Bank of England to explain.

A firm of solicitors in London replied, and told the sad story of a wasted life. Fred came from a good County family, and was really well off. His name was *not* Harrow. He'd studied to take Holy Orders in the Church of England and at the same time passed his music degrees in organ and pianoforte music, had a breakdown in health, and did not go on with the theological studies.

Recovering his health and using his Master's degrees in music, he became a music master at Harrow, the famous English public school—hence the name he had told father.

He eventually lost that position because of bouts of whisky drinking, and became an alcoholic, his family disowned him and sent him out to New Zealand, sending him a remittance from time to time, most of which he spent on whisky.

We learned later that he'd composed some very well-known organ voluntaries and hymn tunes while at Harrow.

I cannot remember much about his movements for a year or so, but he must have been living with us in 1912, because he took my brother and me out to the Heads, (we lived on the Canterbury Coast), to watch the *Terra Nova,* Captain Robert Falcon Scott's little ship, go out through Lyttelton Heads and make for the Antarctic, where Captain Scott would set out for the South Pole and never return. Fred explained to us where this ship was bound for: she was so silvery and small to venture out into the vast South Seas.

I remember old Fred raising his hand as if in blessing, as the *Terra Nova* passed over the horizon, and when we got back to the house, he sat at the piano and played, and we all sang *Eternal Father, Strong to Save,* that lovely old hymn.

I won a bible for a prize at Sunday School and Fred printed my name inside in beautiful Old English lettering. I still treasure it.

I went away to Christchurch to school and do not remember him at our home again. I once asked dad where he was and he said Fred was being well looked after by friends. He died in a Masonic Home during the 1918 influenza epidemic, and father was able to write to his family in England and tell them that Fred was not buried in Potter's Field, but in old Linwood Cemetery, with quite a few friends with some flowers to farewell him, and he had a simple headstone with his real name, and music degree letters after his name.

We all used to go to Christchurch now and then to visit

our grandparents, and we always went, as a family, to put flowers on the graves of relatives, it was part of the visit to Christchurch. We always saved a posy to put in a jam pot on Fred's grave. I can see still my tall 6'5" dad, bare and bow his head and say a prayer for the repose of the soul of Fred the Swagger.

Jack May Swags Today

Jack May swags today, in his mid-sixties, thinking reluctantly of turning it in anytime now at 66, perhaps the last of our fulltime professional swaggers, navy blue beret or felt hat with the brim usually well down on his forehead, swinging a solid beat through Wairarapa, Dannevirke, Manawatu, Rangitikei, King Country, Waimarina, Taihape, Hawkes Bay.

What's he got in his swag? Oh, I did want to know.

"It's what you'd expect: not much different from a hiker's.

"No blankets . . . too heavy. In his bedroll, a couple of overcoats. At night he wears two or three pairs of sox, the overcoats, two jerseys, and as much as he can get on! Sacks

Jack May Swags Today

are too heavy to carry . . . but he'll cover himself with any he finds where he sleeps." Noel Vautier reporting for me.

"Jack spoke of the wonderful blankets chaff bags made years ago. If handy, in the place where he has permission to bunk down overnight, hay bales and a cow cover all help to keep him warm.

"He carries a change of clothing, and this is wrapped in oilskin, to keep dry—but sometimes he has to put wet clothes on again in the morning. This wasn't too bad he said: a good wind on his legs as he walked, and trousers would soon dry.

"Taking emergency cover in an old empty house or shack during a sudden storm sounds simple enough to the layman, but unless you know the chimneys are safe, you daren't light a fire. Perhaps wet clothes are hung to dry a bit near a broken draughty window and it's cold tucker—he may have saved tea in a jar, or thermos.

"He certainly appreciates the value of good boots.

"He keeps food in his 'swag sack', and has the usual tools, such as a tin opener, knife, fork, spoon, cup, billy and so on—just ordinary needs, according to him."

And what's his shakedown like, when he beds down for the night in one of the odd empty cottages where he's got permission to camp in wet weather, here and there on his beat? Jack is always most careful with other people's property, you can make sure of that.

"You'd have loved to see his room in this empty house.

"No furniture, a couple of boxes, and a heap of straw in a corner with two coats turned back like bedclothes. Jack had gathered this straw the first time he slept there, and he carefully ties the door shut with string when he leaves. This is to make sure no cats or animals get in to his room.

"When I called he was having a cold breakfast. The last woman he'd called on had given him sandwiches, cold potatoes, and a tin of sardines. He had some cold tea. I had taken a thermos and boiled eggs and a snack or two down, so he was all right.

"His straw bed looked quite cosy really; I did wonder if there would be any bugs or beetles around, but I don't think that worried Jack. I would say it was as comfortable a place as he'd strike anywhere. Makes me tired to think of walking—walking—really nowhere.

"He was on his way to Hawkes Bay."

One time, Jack covered twenty to even thirty miles in a day, but now he's down to eight or nine miles, at the most. He finds it tiring, his feet hurting now after a long day . . .

But he has that urge to keep going. He doesn't like spending daylight in some particular huts or empty houses because the children throw stones on the roof when they know he is there, and shout at him from the hill behind. Children have always thrown stones at swaggers, particularly when they were trying to sleep, sometimes drunk or painfully recovering from booze, in a hedge or hollow or curled up in the bushes.

Swaggers, almost as much as parents, dreaded the approach of school holidays.

Sometimes Jack May fills in a day under the trees or in some cosy possie reading newspapers or church papers given to him.

Then again, every four or five months, he cuts and trims his beard!

A new experience three years ago was meeting some Pentecostal folk. They gave him a room and told him to stay as long as he liked. He stayed six weeks, savoured the feeling of being wanted, went to some of the meetings, and spoke of the praying and singing into the early hours—the laying on of hands.

"It was a bit too much religion for me," said Jack, but he probably went back there again, religion or not.

Two women wanted to ring the Salvation Army, one trying to find the telephone number there and then.

"But no, don't ring," Jack told her, and she asked:

"Won't you accept a kindness?"

Jack explained he could ring the Salvation Army if he wanted them; all he wanted now was some bread and butter. The housewife gave him two loaves out of her deepfreeze. But her concern for him and her kindness impressed Jack. And there was the vegetarian meal he was invited to share. Not quite filling, but kindness was there, unmistakably.

A woman, providing him with a good breakfast, suddenly startled him when she asked would Jack sit for a sketching class? They'd pay him. He wasn't having that on, he said. So because she'd given him a good breakfast, he let her sketch him, "and she was a real artist."

"My mother is very proud of a portrait in oils she did of Jack May, having it hung in two local exhibitions and receiving favourable comment," wrote Warren Bayliss from Takapau, who photographed him on his beat near Norsewood wearing a navy blue beret and pullover, green corduroy pants, and a brown and white flecked overcoat.

"We are interested in historical things concerning New Zealand," continues Warren, "and in the last couple of years we have built and developed a small local museum to house various items of interest such as moa bones (local), old bottles, photos of local interest, early issues of New Zealand newspapers, and other bits and pieces, and now Jack has an honoured place there."

When the swagger's photograph appeared in the *New Zealand Farmer* soon afterwards, lots of people kept pointing it out to him, pleased he had been noticed, someone so closely and harmlessly part of the countryside.

Told his photograph was now in the Turnbull Library, "he took it in his stride."

He spoke of a brewery van halting beside him, the driver getting out and asking:

"Were you the swagger in the 'Open Country' radio broadcast?"

Jack said he supposed he was.

"I thought you were," said the driver, and got back into his van and drove off.

"And never even offered me a bottle!" said Jack wryly. "So you see it hasn't done me any good."

"In a nutshell, Jack makes his own arrangement regardless of anybody else, also he has decided that it could spoil his image as a swagger to be on radio or TV," sums up Noel Vautier, living a farming life near Feilding. She takes a close and christian interest in Jack. She has interviewed him for me, got answers to questions, taped him, and over a couple of years provided almost all of this chapter. (When baking, she usually makes buns, really enjoys a cup of tea if there's a bun to go with it, and "one day I decided perhaps I'm a bun person.")

Noel continues, and good for them both:

"He said: 'You know, I am the real thing—I am a real swagger.'

"I agreed, but said I thought people would be more interested in him.

" 'No,' said Jack May, repeating it hadn't done him any harm being on radio, but then on the other hand, it hadn't done him any good. The main thing is he feels a real swagger just wouldn't be in the public eye—to such an extent—or through such a medium."

Who is 'a real swagger' then? Certainly holding an honoured place in Jack May's mind is Russian Jack. He admires him. "He's the only one I struck since 1950 on the swag. He kept alone. He really knew how to do it, he was born for the roads."

At least the contents of his swag were the same as Russian Jack's, but a smaller swag. He couldn't carry as much as Russian Jack, who was a much bigger man.

When the mood takes him, occasionally Jack can be silent, or gruff, but: "He can tell you about anything from wars to wool prices," writes another friend and helper Christine Egan, at Rowanbank, thirty miles from Dannevirke. "And no wonder! A neighbour passed him walking along the road, transistor blaring loudly!

"I hope Jack lives as long as another swagger Cockey Wren, from the Woodville area, who died in Dannevirke in October 1972, supposedly about 99 years old!"

He never had any trouble with the law, "just being a swagger on the road—they know me." One policeman, reckoning Jack was getting a bit too threadbare, took him along to the Salvation Army to get outfitted, and Jack was really thrilled. For days afterwards he'd hold out his arms to show people giving him meals how good the suit was. His clothes invariably are too big—Jack is small.

He was offered three suitcases of clothes after a death in one family. "If I'd had a car, I could have taken the lot!"

He stresses the kindness of most people, some with clothes and others with food, which is good to hear, yet the proverbial meanness of some farmers still remains. This example takes some beating. Calling at one farmhouse hoping for breakfast, Jack met the farmer picking up a wire trap containing a live possum caught in the night.

"You can have the possum for breakfast if you like," offered the cockey, holding out the cage.

"No thank you," said Jack quietly, turning on his heel and making off, trying not to feel humiliated.

It's simply not done, to talk or ask about or offer money. Jack avoids the subject, or doesn't reply, and has looked truly pained at times, yet surely a little cash must be handy for him, if given discreetly and diplomatically? Oh yes, a true swagger is not a beggar, as the oldtimers were quick (and often fierce) to point out.

He can always count on a hearty porridge breakfast from one woman, Mrs Burr, who is very good to Jack, remembering how when she was a child her father always insisted every swagger who called must be given a meal, even on the drastic day when eight swaggers were waiting in the yard for dinner, to the despair of her mother:

"I can't possibly supply eight extra men from the meal I've cooked for the family!"

"Well, give them something. They must have something."

In fine and not too cold weather, Jack May sleeps out under trees. For a good deal of the time he travels on sideroads, varying his route somewhat, not liking to call on the same houses too often.

"It's the people who change the roads, as they come and go," says Jack.

How long does a circuit take him? Depending on the weather "and a lot of things," three or four months.

He has been a regular caller at an Ohakune home for about twenty-five years, saying little, sleeping in the shearers' quarters, and "These last few years he has come more often," writes Molly Sommerville, "always very polite, arriving at the house next morning fresh and cleaned up for breakfast. He remembers our children, and is glad to greet their children if they happen to be staying here.

"I sometimes wonder what sort of a childhood he himself had?"

'You've Got To Pocket Your Pride'

Few indeed find even a little brief heaven on this puzzling planet. Most people find a particular hell at times, and the man at war, when filtered to the front, to the awful edge of the battleaxe at last, finds death or disablement in dreadful ways.

Here was a floating hell, all entirely and absolutely man-caused, no demons, no vengeful gods hurling storybook thunderbolts.

All entirely and absolutely man-caused. How long, oh Lord, how long? How long, too, from out of that slaughter would the long red tendons of pain and miseries continue to throb and wince? What long roads of suffering, what blighting of opportunities and lives, began there too? And still the politicians call for sacrifices, "with grave tidings for you, my people," and still admirals and generals speak of freedom while building reputations on pyramids of bones.

HMS Lion was a floating hell, with 99 aboard dead, 44 wounded. This warship, this appalling rat-trap of youth, smashed and fouled like a rubbish-heap tin, was on fire "in half a dozen places; shell fragments had riddled the salt water mains and fire-hoses until it was almost impossible to get water to the flames, some of which roared up from powder-fires of terrific intensity. Since the beginning of the action *Lion* had been struck thirteen times by heavy shells. The main and gun-decks were littered with tangled wreckage; dead and wounded men lay everywhere through the batteries; electric lighting had been blown away—dim lanterns and flickering flames lit the smoky stinking interiors."

Slain, or drowned in this shambles were 6,274 British sailors, 2,545 German sailors, history's biggest naval battle at Jutland in the merry month of May, 1916.

"Inconclusive," said the British historians. "Victory," claimed German historians.

Strangely enough *HMS New Zealand,* a battle cruiser playing an undistinguished part and carrying Maori curios, escaped virtually without injury. This ship was bought for the British Navy as a gift by the people of New Zealand from money borrowed in London. She was commissioned in 1913, declared obsolete only eleven years later, was stripped down, towed to deep water, and sunk.

We finished paying the bill of £3,412,682 for this ship, (when the average New Zealand factory worker's wage over one week in 1929 was £4/10/1 ($9.00) for men and £1/19/6 ($4.00) for women) on 1 November 1929, just in time for the Great Depression.

Among those 8,819 dead sailors at Jutland lay an English sailor named May, sprawled among the broken dead on *HMS Lion.*

Soon after this his wife died. The children were orphans now, so into an orphanage with them, until young Jack May, at the age of 14, with a brother, was sent out to New Zealand in 1924, to Flock House.

Why Flock House?

The place, and this was its first year, was a scheme pioneered by New Zealand sheepowners to give sons of British seamen who died in World War 1 a chance to train in agriculture. When numbers dwindled, the New Zealand Government took over in 1937.

A distinctive training farm for youths, Flock House, near Bulls, is run by the Ministry of Agriculture and Fisheries, a big property, 1133 hectares, with four separate farm units: dairy, fat lamb, mixed cropping, and all-beef. Flock House gives a one-year course in brains and brawn on the farm for 60 young men aged from 16 to 18, the days starting at 6.30 a.m., sometimes 5.30 a.m.

Jack spent six months at Flock House, learning the ways and customs of a new land as well as something about the toils and trials of agriculture.

He worked in Northland for two years on a mixed farm, then to near Levin on a dairy farm. His brother returned to Britain during the depression, and the remains of the family lost touch. Apparently the last links had been broken.

You've Got to Pocket Your Pride 97

War came again.

Jack did not volunteer: "I'll wait till they come for me."

They did, all right, inevitably, and at the age of 31, passed medically fit, no trouble—eyes, feet, 'Now cough'—Jack entered the Army in January, 1942.

The first six weeks in peaceful Plimmerton on coastal defence defending Wellington which remained unconquered, then for another six weeks in those hustling barking stockyards of Trentham Military Camp, then as winter approached, away to Fiji, over the sea growing purple or violet coloured with the flying fish leaping by the lovely lace at the bow.

Six weeks in Fiji, among the hibiscus, the Sultan-like coconut palms particularly dramatic at night against a moonwashed sky, the sweating soldiers learning to say 'Bula', singing *Isa Lei,* drinking kava ceremoniously from a large turtle-shell bowl among the oil-smelling shadows of kerosene lamp lit grass huts, feeling homesick, wandering slowly away when the mail was given out, aching unexpectedly for a handful of gooseberries or a crisp Granny Smith or Cox's Orange instead of pineapples which made your gums sore and passionfruit like golfballs, cursing the mosquitoes, the hornets big as tiger-hued sparrows to the reluctantly awakening glazed eye focusing onto them hovering three feet away around the ginger-blossom lei brought back and hung above the humble Army bed during the drunken night before, cursing the mangroves *and* the swamps, the wasted weeks and the coral sores and the sergeant major, the obscene toads, the Army, the war, the liquid bully beef, and the recoiling horrors gnarled Army cooks, conscripted from unimaginable wallows and penal stations, fashioned in delirium tremens from the tops and bulbs of innocent taro . . .

Moved to the mud and heat and boredom of the Solomon Islands for two years and two actions, where everyone said: "Gee, I only wish I was back in Fiji again," Jack May was directed back to Europe once more by way of Egypt briefly, then Bari Base Camp near the heel of Italy, then to the Po Valley, and the last big advance towards Trieste in early 1945, when his unit suffered unnerving casualties—nobody wants to be killed in a war, least of all when the war itself is obviously dying.

Jack collected a very slight wound in a finger, "scarcely worth bothering about," he didn't go and get medical attention, the endless war ended, he took three weeks on a fortnight's leave to cross France to England, and hunt up his brother, who had married, and his two sisters; then away back south, to New Zealand, and the attempt to become a civilian again.

But his heart wasn't in it.

"After the war, I seemed to lose ambition, and the will to go on."

The customary routine was not for him anymore, and in 1950 he took up swagging, seriously, professionally, for good.

As he began, he asked a swagger for advice about the business of approaching homes. How could you tell a good place from a bad place, and what to do?

"You've got to find out for yourself. Learn by experience, it's the only way," the swagger told him. Jack soon learned.

The passing miles and months began to clean and free him from this tyranny of possessions, a cancer of the 20th century. With this, money itself began to mean even less to him. He'd opted out of "this mania for owning things," as Walt Whitman had deplored.

Yet when someone rebuffs you, or is particularly rude or coarse, or sarcastic, the dog snarling? What then?

"If it's a bad place, why you just don't call again, that's what."

He himself sums the whole thing up with:

"You've got to pocket your pride when you go up to people to ask for a handout."

His life in some ways can be compared with a commercial traveller, moving on . . . different places . . . a beat . . .

He may get a room in a year or so and settle in . . . "and then get the Universal (pension), that's an excuse I know, but still . . ." but he's not too keen on it: still is lured by and likes the open air and road.

And when the thunder rolls about the hills, does that

solitary figure, I wonder, ever find himself briefly thinking about Jutland, his father, and how *and why* it all began?

But for me, enough of the butcher's block called Europe, the South is calling.

Off, and inland the noble way by the Rainbow Trail, through the great hills and the great stations where the great mobs of sheep passed, where a chopwhiskered old coot planted fruit stones and pips wherever he could, where one day legends thick as mushrooms will tell of drovers and sheepmen, tremendous women with football-team folded arms and breasts like Tapuaenuku (no! *not* like tapioco!), and the shy governess who flattened the lot, of packmen, sheepdogs, crazed cattle, cooks, hacks and rabbiters, docking and dagging and dipping and dunnies, wild pigs and the Matagouri Ghost, shearers, painkiller, ploughmen, fencers and the bolder swagger men shouldering along the skyline!

Russian Jack Vos Beautiful!

What excitement, the night Russian Jack stayed at our place! We were living on a dairyfarm in the Wairarapa. I came round the carshed corner after the evening milking, my mind on the meal cooking away inside the kitchen, and there to my surprise was Russian Jack, sitting on the back doorstep! (How pleased I was when Elva J. Sonntag sent this account to me. As time passes I like more and more her description of this brief visit, comfortably placing the reader alongside this lonely wanderer, a sympathetic piece of human countryside history. The humble and meek will be remembered.)

Russian Jack, the swagger, at our place—this really was something. The children were hovering around excitedly.

"Good-day, Missus," he said cheerily. "Your man's fillin' me billy."

A tall well-built figure, he had a drooping Stalin-like moustache. He always wore a wide-brimmed felt hat, and this was swinging on top of the walking-stick propped up alongside him. His pack, inevitably with a shining billy tied to it, was missing. He always carried a huge pack, and a sugarbag crammed with odds and ends.

"Can sleep calf-shed by gate, missus, please?" asked this so aged yet ageless man. "M'pack's back down road. I get it if I can."

He had quite an accent. His speech was in any case not very distinct, but asking to sleep in the calf-shed bothered me. This rough shelter stood on the side of the road, small and not properly waterproof. The bobby calves waited in it when the lorry came to collect them in the springtime. In any case, it seemed awful to have any guest sleeping in a shed.

But Russian Jack went on reassuringly: "Won't be any trouble, missus. If rains I stay in shed all day, dry." And then, turning to our young son Andrew: "Don't be frightened, sonny—I just having rest. M'feet very sore."

Andrew was grinning delightedly. Frightened? Not likely. Just wait till he told the kids about this at school tomorrow!

We'd heard about Jack staying at places in the district before. He made fairly regular spring and autumn calls to the Wairarapa, and we'd often seen him making his way over the rough Pahiatua Track (the road over the Tararuas from the Wairarapa to the Manawatu). News would come quickly from the school.

"Russian Jack's back," they'd say. "He's been two nights now in the old shack by the creek down the way."

The old stories went the rounds—speculation about who he really was, how long he'd been a swagger, and so on.

He'd been walking the roads for half a century. He'd had only a little schooling in his native Latvia. He'd gone to sea at twenty-four, and the chance shipwreck of the steamer *Star of Canada* on the Gisborne coast in 1912 put him ashore and on to the New Zealand roads for keeps. His restlessness became his way of life, until his death after three years in an old folks' home in Greytown on 19 September, 1968.

Now he was visiting us. I asked my husband on the quiet what he thought about letting him sleep in a shed. Like all farmhouses, ours had had its share of visitors over the years, but none had ever had to sleep in a shed.

"Don't you think we should make up a bed in some place for him?"

My husband didn't think so. We were living on the farm where he'd grown up. Swaggers had visited frequently in years gone by.

"They love it out of doors," he said. "He'd never be happy in a bed."

However, we did talk the old chap into coming nearer the house, into the warmer shed where we stored superphosphate in season.

Making Russian Jack understand what we had to say was very difficult. He seemed so deaf. I sat down on the step for a minute to tell him: "Did you know your photo has been in the paper?"

"Eh, vot's dat, missus?"

I tried miming reading the paper. "Newspaper—*The Dominion* you know—a photo of you in the paper."

"'Ave I got some py-pa, missus?" he replied, perplexed.

I gave up trying to make him understand what a character he was becoming. He just lived his own life, unimpressed by any words, written or otherwise.

There'd been an excellent photo of him preparing his own fern-and-twig version of a roadside motel. Someone was hunting frantically for the old newspaper as I tried to explain to him but we never found it.

Offered a meal, he understood all right, but he'd got some bread in town as he passed through Pahiatua. That would be enough, unless we had some meat.

"I like meat," he said.

I showed him some uncooked fry.

"Goodt, goodt, I like very much."

One of the family offered to get his pack, but he preferred to collect it himself. It looked such a heavy load. By the time he got back his meal was cooked.

He washed most thoroughly in the bathroom, and the hand towel he brought with him was very clean. Almost ceremoniously he wrapped it round his head. This intrigued me. He seemed to want his head covered as he ate. Jewish friends of ours told us this was their custom. I wondered, could he be Jewish? I set down his meal and he obviously enjoyed it, but he didn't seem to want to linger.

"I think I go lie down now," he said, "M'feet very sore. I rest."

He tapped the aged boots together quite sharply; then once or twice more.

"Helps stop py'n bit, missus," he said.

I felt sad for him. Surely he deserved a more comfortable end to his working and walking days. But he was singing happily as he rounded the carshed.

A little later, one of the children came in, panicky, saying: "I can smell smoke. He's burning down our shed!"

I knew this wasn't likely, because Russian Jack stayed regularly at places all over Wellington province and he was by reputation most careful of other people's property.

But I slipped out, just in case. It was really rather eerie. We could hear him chattering loudly in what seemed like another language. The sound seemed to fill the air. Then he stopped abruptly.

"It's *prayers*," said Pamela in excited awe.

"Yes," agreed Philip, "I heard him say 'table' and 'nightfall'."

We were intruders. Tonight outside was his. He started singing happily again.

"Fancy being happy like that under those horrible sacks," wondered young Andrew. "I'd itch like mad." Andrew had watched his dad make up a bed of sacks for the old chap.

Next morning, as we passed by on our way to the cowshed, our visitor was just a sacky hump, but by calf-feeding time he was up and asking for water for a wash.

I pointed to his feet. "Better?" I asked.

"Sometimes, missus, they so sore—can't stand on 'em."

"You should see a doctor," I tried to say. It was all so difficult.

"Can I bandage them for you?" I asked. Then I suggested: "Would you stay here a while?"

He could understand enough to tell me: "No, barnages no goodt."

The only way to help seemed to be provisions for the trip to the next stopping place.

Yes, eggs were good, "Boil them, missus," and the tea comes in handy. The offer of cigarettes delighted him.

"Very goodt, very goodt!" he said, beaming.

He had breakfast and made ready to go. He shook our hands enthusiastically.

"It vos beautiful, beautiful!" he said.

I just never had a nicer thank you from a visitor.

Russian Jack was ready for the road again.

'Man Oh Man, I Vos Free!'

"I got firm rememberies. I don't pick them up again. My swaggering days are over now."

In 53 years swagging in the North Island he'd been everywhere except New Plymouth. In Auckland someone stole ten shillings from him while he slept. He never went back to that wicked city again!

Like a snail carrying its home on its back, the fabled Russian Jack had in his swag blankets, two towels, underwear and other clothing including two or three pairs of boots, potatoes—"Everything was in there"— a billy, and two tins of dripping. He rubbed dripping onto his chest "to keep away itches." Sometimes he rubbed a spoonful of dripping into his neck.

He had the bluest, clearest eyes you have ever seen.

"Oh man! Them days vos everydays happy. Ha ha!"

"Thirty years ago," he told one Wairarapa woman, as he passed by on his way, "I say: 'To hell with work and worry.' I go on the road."

Born in Latvia 26 March 1878, he had three years schooling in a little place called Alexandra, working in scrubcamps (presumably some elementary forestry work but this could well be confused with scrubcutting he did when stranded in New Zealand) and at the age of twenty-four set out from home to be a sailor and see the world.

Ten years later he landed up in a shipwreck off Gisborne when the British ship *Star of Canada* came to grief on the coast on Sunday 3 June, 1912.

Years later, an old man, almost stone deaf now, he became greatly excited when a friendly Masterton journalist T. F.

Collerton showed him a photograph of a house in Gisborne, "part of which has been made from the upper works of the *Star of Canada*. He looked at it for some half minute then exclaimed:

" 'My ship—my ship!' "

The doomed ship had dragged its anchor in the storm, and obeying orders and struggling to help free the other anchor, Jack was nearly swept away in the waves beating down.

His name, or the name he gathered very probably as a member of the crew, was Barrett Crumen, [Barret Krumen in the hospital records] explains the journalist, "as he put it:

" 'Ivan what you call Jack.'

"I never succeeded to my satisfaction in getting his surname. 'Barrett', his name recorded in the hospital books, seemed to mean nothing spelt out or spoken to him—but then it is somewhat difficult to talk to a man who has a far from perfect command of English and has both ears packed with wadding soaked in mutton fat 'to keep the bugs out'.

"Anyhow, after this shipwreck, Crumen decided to save on coach fares by walking to Wellington," where he probably intended to sign on in another ship, "but in the highways and byways of rural Hawkes Bay and the Wairarapa, he became a swagger. Before long, his marked Russian accent led to his nickname 'Russian Jack'."

Remember that 'Russian Jack' was a general name for anyone on the road, possibly of Russian descent, who couldn't be understood very well: New Zealand had at least two other 'Russian Jack's'.

> "Man oh man I vos FREE! Free to have a beer, have a smoke—happy what you can call all the time, you know. They was free days."

"A big upstanding man," "a powerful man," "a fine figure of a man, fresh healthy complexion," people say, then pause, remembering him again as "considerably shrunken" after thirty to forty years on the roads.

"His clothes eventually became so patched, he looked as if he was covered with pockets, a striking figure, cleanshaven except for a moustache, and no sideboards," writes one Rangitikei countrywoman.

His boots too, incredibly worn and twisted and patched with bits of tyres as his years on the road drew to a close: they may be seen today in Wanganui Regional Museum, the gift of a Turakina farmer K. E. Reynolds, who also handed over an autograph Jack did for him in pencil on a fence paling: 'Bernet Kruman'.

"The boots, which weigh eight and a half pounds," writes the museum director D. W. Cimino, "have been repeatedly repaired with thick scraps of leather and rubber, attached by ordinary carpenter's nails. They are lined inside with paper and corrugated cardboard, and the distorted shape is probably responsible for the foot-trouble which landed him into the Greytown hospital."

"The cook would carve two helpings from a shoulder of mutton and hand Jack the rest; same with the pudding. A huge man even when he was older and a very gentle, kindly person," writes James L. Fraser of Napier, a workmate when Jack was in his prime before the First World War. James continues:

"Russian Jack's Wairarapa possie was Awhea Station, or Stony Creek as it was more often called. Jack turned up around September and he cut tawhiny till the docking started. The Manager, Simon Campbell, was very good to Jack. He had his own hut known as Jack's hut. Jack held lambs then till shearing began, when he went on the press—and great wool too, over 400 bales went out.

"Tremendously strong, he was just the man for the job. One day he and his mate were struggling to put down a heavy bale of bellies when Jack's lever broke. He was hurled against the wall, severely bruising one side of his face and head.

"Along the famous gale-swept Range Road a gig was blown over the side, no damage, nobody hurt, so the boss sent three men, including Jack, up to get it back on the road. Jack took the shafts, the other two pushed, and away they went. Halfway up one pusher said: 'I wonder how much Jack could really pull? Let's hang back.'

"But old Jack was equal to it, the wheels kept rolling."

Around Palmerston North they remember how in the spring when the ewes were lambing he would return from the Wairarapa wearing a warm woollen overcoat looking fit and well on his way north to the Rangitikei district.

When autumn came round again he would pass through Ashhurst and travel by the Aokautere-Pahiatua track road over the Range back to the Wairarapa. A nearby farmer "who had known Russian Jack with that heavy swag close on 40 years," never saw him ever tramping through the Manawatu Gorge, and here's another place he apparently avoided:

"The swagger told me that he was in the Hawkes Bay area at the time of the Napier earthquake, 3 February 1931, and he never returned to the Bay after that.

"With the increase in motor traffic on the roads he seemed charmed to escape being hit by a passing car. Russian Jack seemed to outlive them all."

"I take some lifts in cars. Not very many," he had told people.

Late in 1946 an old Essex car containing a padre from 18 Battalion 2NZEF and his newly-wed nursing-sister wife pulled up to offer a lift on the road between Tiraumea and Pongaroa, northern Wairarapa. "He had little conversation, smelt a bit—mainly of smoke and lack of soap—but seemed grateful, and knew where he wanted to get off," noted the driver, padre R. M. (Pat) Gourdie, who twenty years later as Vicar of Greytown would meet him again in Buchanan Ward, with "his invariable greeting: 'Good day mister', said in strange clipped tones." Reverently he sat on his bed during Sunday afternoon church service in the Men's Ward not uttering a word. Later, "it fell to my lot—no, honour," to conduct his funeral service.

"First ride in motorcar when I was in Wellington. I was drunk! And arrested" (on other occasions) *"too*

for it! One night I was drunk and what the devil to do? I'm in fright I might get arrested again."

Sonia Mackenzie of Puketapu, living in the Makuri area, had him calling regularly about three times a year in his elderly years. He asked only for two things: a billy of tea, or, "Any spare dripping, missus?"

"On inquiry, he told us he used the dripping to cook possums in his billy!

"However one cold wet winter morning he called and joined us at breakfast, as there were spare chops in the pan.

"Well! I could hardly eat at all, for when he removed his battered felt hat, on his head sat a greasy circle of many layers of brown wrapping paper, which sat firmly no matter how he moved.

"I was fascinated, but waited in vain for the 'cap' to fall into his breakfast."

> "There was motorcar by Trocadero Hotel just two or three chain away from Mr and Mrs Fox's backyard," (where he used to camp in Wellington). "I had some money given to me, I give the driver half a crown, I hop in, he take me two or three chain to the Fox's backyard—my first ride in motorcar!"

The Ponatahi round was one of his regular beats, Dick Hewitt seeing him staying next door to 'Taratanui'. Sometimes he would camp under the Kokotau bridge for a few days, the settlers giving him some stores or the odd hot meal. He'd make his way out to Castlepoint and the coast, too. The station owner and M.P. Sir George Hunter was interested in swaggers and at times had quite a gathering bunking down. Some say he looked after them extra well to get the odd vote!

Another family last saw Jack sitting resting in an old metal quarry by the road at Kakariki, "and I still see him there every time I pass . . ."

"He used to be seen on the Para-Paras as well," records Mrs R. Earnshaw of New Plymouth, raised in Martinborough and confirming Jack's appetite in his working days when he could put away a whole leg of mutton plus a good many boiled eggs at one meal. "He was a tailor made man, only one of his kind ever made."

He favoured most oddly a square billy.

"He had a thing about his billy being immaculate on the inside. His cleanliness was a characteristic," says Creina Draper of Pahiatua. "The material blocking his ears had an acorn-look, it was so aged, making conversation virtually impossible, similar to those old ones who live in blissful peace because their hearing aids are turned off!"

Many children treated him with reserve, apprehension, awe: "He'd sit on the side of the road and the kids remember skirting-around him wondering if he'd say anything to them and some of them crossing over to the fence line on the other side of the road for a quick getaway if necessary."

The children of at least one Wairarapa school did a project on him, exhibiting drawings on the schoolhouse walls. Bert Ihaka, retired farmworker, of Masterton, in 1972 carved in totara wood an eleven-inch statue of Russian Jack, complete with stick, billy and swag.

"He carried the biggest swag I've ever seen any man carry," Bert told a *Times-Age* reporter. "He was a pathetic figure in his last days on the road around 1965. One foot was bent over and he walked on the side of it. He must have been made of iron to live the way he did."

One sustaining comfort was tobacco, 'Silver Fern' was good, but preferably pipe tobacco for a venerable pipe he'd puff briefly, thrust a cork into the bowl, then return to his pocket.

The last person you could call a bludger, goodnatured and courteous, Russian Jack always swept out and tidied up any hut he was allowed to sleep or camp in. He kept little bivouacs or shelters of branches and tin with perhaps some hay for a carpet in some places round the countryside, "hanging an old billy at the entrance to catch rainwater, always a sure sign that Jack was 'at home'," noticed Elva J. Sonntag.

"At nights he stuffed his clothing with old newspapers to keep out the bitter cold, and his ears were always stuffed with rag or paper wads to prevent aches."

The pain increased. His remaining strength ebbed away. Admitted to Pahiatua Hospital with frostbite of the feet, he was transferred to Greytown Hospital on 2 July 1965.

Nationality: Lett or Latvian, a member of the Lutheran Church. He said he had no relatives or friends to be notified about illness or death.

"My swaggering has finished now. Yes. Finished. So I'm now say good-bye."

"An old man with a serene expression, slow movements and a kindly manner: how long would he stay, would the call of the road when springtime came be irresistible to him? I think he realized that the years had taken their toll, and his pace had slowed down." These were the impressions of Dr C. D. Banks, Medical Superintendent of Greytown Hospital for 25 years, when Russian Jack was admitted to Buchanan Ward.

"When admitted," continued the doctor, "he had several layers of brown paper against his chest under his clothing, and it was some weeks before he could be persuaded to part with it. More strange was his habit of stuffing both ears with brown paper and mutton fat, and this habit we never succeeded in breaking (we didn't try very hard!). This increased his deafness, so with the language difficulty thrown in, communication was difficult. But there was always that slow, friendly smile until one tried to take the brown paper from his ears.

"He showed little animation after his admission here, except on one occasion when a reporter came to interview him and produced a photograph of Jack's old ship, wrecked near Gisborne in 1912.

" 'Dat's my ship!' said he, displaying the most animation we had seen since he was admitted."

"Yes man I got to stay here," (*chuckling warmly*) *"can't get away! I got to go by all that, I can't do nothing else. I lay down on the bed no more road to do."*

Everyone liked the old man, who was up and about most of the time. The authorities and nurses on the quiet rather enjoyed making a fuss of him, and his many sudden requests for a tin so he could boil the billy! He was allowed to keep his swaggering-days stick under the bed. Someone in Wellington regularly sent him peppermints.

A good smiling patient, "but when he didn't want to speak he couldn't, and when he didn't want to listen he was deaf!"

"So these days surrendered. No more happy. When I'm dead and gone, first happy be in next world. First mate I meet, I'm together again, same as other man. That be the happiest time for me."

Three years later, on 19 September 1968, aged 90, Russian Jack went west.

"He died after a short illness of only four days—gently and quietly, as he had lived," wrote Dr Banks.

"I have retained a vivid impression of his ancient face lit with the gentle eyes of innocence," writes Matron G. Pattulle. "He had the trust of a child that the world is full of kindness—and maybe this had been his armour throughout the long years."

On his coffin lay a great wreath of spring blossoms from the staff and patients.

His accumulated pension paid for his funeral. Reports saying he was buried in a pauper's grave are untrue. Until admission to hospital, Russian Jack had never claimed a pension. Until the age of 87 years, he had never cost the State a cent.

"This could apply to many old swaggers," points out Matron Pattulle, "who although considered itinerant 'beggars', had their own fierce independence."

Because he'd attended in turn all the different religious services in the hospital, they held the funeral service in the Methodist Church with an Anglican minister, the Reverend

R. M. Gourdie, and at the graveside a Presbyterian took over, the Reverend J. N. McDougall. A good number came to pay their respects, one family from as far away as Waipukurau. An old soldier, who did not write again, J. A. N. King of Pukekohe, sent a letter to the hospital, offering to pay for a headstone with a brass plaque.

He was buried in the Greytown lawn cemetery, where a simple cross marks his grave. Fresh flowers are still laid there, in memory, from time to time.

One of the six pallbearers, Collerton the journalist, remarked:

"The words of the final hymn provided a fitting epitaph:

> "O spread Thy covering wings around till all our wanderings cease, and at our Father's loved abode our souls arrive in peace."

Women Concerned

New Zealand still has a woman swagger. Peggy Dunstan now tells how, at the Wellington railway station in July 1970, she met her, neat but tense (her feet didn't seem to fit into modern civilization), slung with five small haversacks (not a swag) an old battered cardboard suitcase, a rug and three coats.

She was blackhaired, not a grey hair, beautifully spoken, very dark eyes, brown complexion, aged around 40, wearing slacks and brogues, live, muscular but lithe, long-legged, and detesting train travel.

She'd walked down from Napier, never hitch-hiked, and was going by rail to Masterton to see a sick friend, dreading the trip and the night she'd possibly have to sleep inside.

Then back to the road, sending her suitcase on ahead, her only concession.

Renting a little place in Wellington to store winter or summer clothing (when out of season) and a few books, she had three different sets of sandshoes, changing into them during the day and so avoiding hot and blistered feet, the curse of footsloggers. I was earnestly assured this was vitally necessary for foot-travel.

She'd sleep outside when it wasn't raining—when wet, on verandahs, in sheds, or under any cover offering—once even cramming herself into a milkstand until the storm passed.

She had a well-worked-out and most satisfactory beat, which took her 16 to 18 months to complete, never going further north than Hamilton, and covering much of the South Island before winter.

She loathed a roof over her head, feeling stifled and imprisoned.

What would start a woman out on the roads like this?

At school she'd failed School Certificate, went to her brother's farm in North Otago, quarrelled, and decided to hike to another farm 40 miles away. Once there, and under a roof, she decided this was not for her and took to the roving life for good, full-time, except for the odd brief job, and occasional fruitpicking and tobacco grading.

I'd love to meet her again.

Do you remember the impact and longing of Rat, in *The Wind In The Willows,* meeting a swagger rat who was up and away adventuring once more as spring came swirling in? The outdoors lure our Otago woman obeyed is felt by two girls (who knows, will they fully succumb one day?) Noel Vautier met near Feilding:

One late afternoon, we picked up two girls who said they were looking for a haystack to sleep in. Rather horrified, we told them there were no haystacks in this area.

They had hitch-hiked to Auckland to attend some Navy Ball, and now were hitch-hiking to Wellington where they worked.

As we came closer to our turnoff to Feilding, I suggested they come home with us for the night.

They wouldn't hear of this.

One of the girls spoke to me, so nicely, almost as if speaking to a child: "Don't worry about us—we can look after ourselves—we are used to this."

We left them, but instead of walking on, they turned back up the hill we'd come down. They were evidently going to spend the night in the Mount Stewart Memorial on top of the hill, and if that did not suit, there were large macrocarpa trees down the bank off the side of the road.

I did understand, town girls wanting to sleep under the stars.

A woman swagger lived on for many years in the mind of a farmer in Canterbury, where Mrs Antonio, the Syrian swagger, pushed her pack in a pram: "She must have had a constitution like a tugboat!" The one this man remembered best above all others was Annie Stander:

"She was goodlooking in her younger days, a fierce kind of beauty. I still remember Annie's remark: 'I often say that Captain Cook deserves to be tommyhawked for discovering these Islands!' "

The only woman swagger Dan Greaney of Jackson Bay ever saw was at Dannevirke in about 1928. From the first floor of the post office he looked out into the street and there were these two swaggers, side by side heading south, the woman with a smaller swag and—incredibly—in knee-high gumboots, and in hot summer, too.

A week later, and the same two again, returning, making for Napier now, and both drunk, reeling into each other.

"I couldn't blame her, and still in those gumboots too."

"That old Assyrian woman," (as everyone referred to her) used to call at Mavis Matthew's small town in Southland pushing an ancient pram loaded with odds and ends for sale.

One very wet day, one of her customers, a most religious woman whose back door had no shelter, said to her:

"I don't want anything today—but I'd like to have a little talk to you about your soul. Do you know the Lord?"

To this, the old woman replied: "Yes Ma'am. I do know the Lord. In fact, He's a fellow-countryman of mine.

"I know the Lord well enough to know He wouldn't keep a poor old woman standing in the rain while He talked about her soul."

The housewife quickly apologized, saying they'd have to talk another day, and it was she who told the story against herself.

Loud knockings on the back door (mother and I alone, father away in Christchurch, writes D. A. Goss, Havelock North). This swagger looked quite frightening, unshaven and unkempt and muttering very incoherently to mother holding the kerosene lamp. He was trembling, too.

The poor old chap's feet were sore and blistered and inclined to bleed. He was carrying one very old tennis shoe and wearing the other—and he was kind of whimpering like a sick animal.

Mum sat him on the woodbox at the back door, got a large basin of warm water ready, and soon the poor old tramp fellow was soaking his sore feet in heavenly warm soapy water and had stopped whimpering—his sad, tired eyes were following my mother like a faithful dog as she made him a huge cold meat sandwich and a brew of tea.

He began to look human again, and was given a big jug of buttermilk, a great hunk of sultana cake, and told to make himself comfy in the trap shed with clean chaff sacks and a cover.

I can still see mother next kneeling (and this was in 1910), drying his feet, patting them with a towel, so as not to hurt him, rubbing his feet with some oil, giving them a lavish sprinkling of some mysterious powder known as Fuller's Earth, and giving him a clean pair of dad's handknitted socks and an awfully old pair of carpet slippers.

Later, when I was old enough to understand readings from the bible, whenever I heard the story of a woman washing and drying Jesus's feet for Him, I could picture my mother kneeling washing His feet instead of the poor old swagger's.

Nora Sanderson was sitting alone in the kitchen one

evening knitting baby clothes when the door handle began stealthily to turn.

This was during The Great Depression of the 1930s, she writes, when my husband and I occupied the Havelock parsonage on the main Blenheim-to-Nelson route. The swaggers who came to the door were courteous and appreciative but I was not happy about our frequent callers when my husband was away down the Sounds for a week at a time.

So this night, I crept out the front door and brought over my neighbour to face the intruder—which turned out to be nothing worse than an opossum hanging by its tail from the door handle.

The policeman then knocked at the door. He'd come to tell me he would be staying with the five swaggers camped in the empty house next door until they settled down for the night.

I was very touched by his kindness, but perhaps even more touched by what followed next morning. I was in the yard splitting kindling for the fire when one of the swaggers came through and took the axe from me.

"A woman in your condition shouldn't be chopping wood," he said, and proceeded to pile up a great heap of kindling wood for me. Moreover, he refused even a cup of tea before setting out along the road, his swag on his back.

Diana Greensill, also of the Sounds, tells of two Irish rovers, certainly restless, but one at least working a little too much to be a true-blue swagger:

Mick was string-lean, with long Irish upper lip and with him went Muggins, so exactly the right shaggy humorous part-beardy dog to be a wandering Irishman's companion. We all liked Mick and were glad when we heard, at the kitchen door, his soft beguiling Irish voice greeting us:

"Good-day, missus, very comical weather we're having."

Things were just a little bit extra when he was around, and we all tried to lure him on to the payroll; but he would not settle, and soon drifted on, his long legs in faded denims scissoring up the miles.

"Good-day to you missus," he'd say. "I won't see you again till you can see me."

Paddy, accompanied by his partner Mutto, a grizzled beardie-type sheepdog, could turn his hand to anything.

He was a good stockman, tireless with grubber or slasher, a handy carpenter; he could milk the cows, shoe a horse, set a broody hen, sole a pair of boots, or take a swarm of bees, and, talking quietly in his soft Irish voice, soothe an enraged baby.

But Paddy couldn't settle. No blandishments, neither flattery nor another rise in pay—or even, in one case, the offer of the farmer's sister-in-law's hand in marriage—could tempt the restless Paddy to stay longer. He'd be over the hills and far away . . .

Christina Macdonald, of Two Thumb Range, tells how swaggers would come to the back door, or at a bigger farm to the cookhouse, ask for food and shelter for the night, and offer to chop kindling, or do some digging (very seldom this one!).

Swaggers were a varied lot of men, all ages, all sizes. Some just had a wanderlust, some a drink problem, others an inability to stick to any job.

Some were of a better type—I knew one who was the author of several books and carried copies in his swag. He made his living by selling them at the stations as he passed through.

Others were nature lovers, and these used to entrance us when we were children with their knowledge of the ways of birds, rabbits, weasels, fish, and weather signs.

My father always looked at their boots, and they went away with a better pair if their own were literally 'on their uppers'.

They left signs for each other, copied somehow from the gypsies of Europe. These signs were stones placed in certain ways, or a mark on the gate itself, to let those following know that it was either a good or a bad place to approach.

They have no place in today's world, those loners who were free and independent of any restriction on their coming and going, and whose worst enemy was winter.

To the North Island, to Feilding, to Noel Vautier again:

Unless you see a swagger reasonably often you can't know much about him personally. I think of earlier days when, like bits of driftwood, they came and disappeared.

"Have you got a bone, lady?" or "Have you a crust to spare, missus?"

This last request recalls a very angry swagger, for someone had told him that morning she had no bread, and he saw "a great hunk in her scrap-tin that I would have been glad to have," he told me.

And the saddest of them all, the signwriter who held up shaking hands: "This is what the war did to me," and looking at his feet: "Me poor feet."

I saw him some years later in Awapuni Home where old and disabled folk go. Many others are memories, faded as old photos.

While I never ever refused food, I was young, and wonder now if I fully understood the tragedy of many of these men.

Noel Vautier's swagger angered over the bread discarded in the scrap-tin has an echo one Christmas Day as the floodwaters subsided, writes Phyllis Sloan, Te Puke. This swagger walked kneedeep through the water to the nearest house and asked the housewife: "For the good Lord's sake lady, give me a crust of bread and a drink of water."

To the swagger's surprise she obliged him with exactly what he had requested.

"For Christ's sake Mum, put a bit of butter on it!" burst from his lips, but with the words: "Oh you wicked man!" ringing in his ears he decided to try the next door neighbours for his Christmas crust.

Shaking, groaning, holding his jaw, and begging for methylated spirits to fix his dreadful 'teethick', Old Bluey, unkempt and fearsome looking with bushy very-red hair and walrus moustache, startled and briefly mystified the young Belgian bride of Jack O'Malley, a 1914-18 soldier-farmer near the south bank of the Rakaia River.

"Eventually he opened his mouth very wide and pointed inside with a particularly grubby finger. What a ghastly sight—I could not see a vestige of a tooth in that terrible cavern, but he kept insisting on meths for his 'teethick'."

Very purposefully, the farmer's wife strode inside to her well-stocked medicine cupboard (the sudden demands of shearing and harvesting, and toothache was very common then), returned with medicine bottle and spoon in hand, and as Old Bluey the swagger "opened his mouth to protest, flung inside a full dessertspoonful of the good old cure, oil of cloves."

As a mere drop of this fiery stuff on cotton wool usually 'drowns the toothache' immediately, Bluey sprang into action and bolted like a cut cat through the yard gate, just as the men came in for smoko to rear with laughter and explain Bluey was a metho, and wanted a bottle of meths—*to drink!*

An innocent Amazon wordlessly sent another swagger speeding on his way, like this. N. F. Wheeler's young aunt dashed out the back door and in amazement saw a terrified looking tramp rushing out the garden gate and continuing full-tilt until out of sight.

Completely bewildered she gazed after him—and then realised her menacing attitude, holding aloft a large piece of wood too big for the fire box which she had meant to heave back into the wheelbarrow! Clearly he thought he was about to be shown violently off the premises!

The Devil at the door, in female or male shape—but it takes more than that to perturb a good commonsense nurse, such as Winifred Read, of Sumner:

My peace in the country hospital was shattered when Sister and the senior nurse burst through the swing doors with, what so far as I could gather, a statement that the Devil was at the front door! There was a noise, you could hear the chains clanking, the rattle of hooves, and in the feeble torchlight there indeed were the horns and red eyes!

I'd never seen the Devil, and with some doubts that they had either, we went back to the front door the three of us. When the light was switched on, there was old Kirkman the swagger flat on the doormat—and dancing around him his goat.

Between us we lifted him in and on to a bed and shut the door on the goat.

The doctor, quite a character himself, decided the old man had had a heart attack, and as he had an irregular heart beat, could do with some treatment and a spell of warmth and care.

I knew who this abrupt visitor was all right: one of the regulars who had stayed at what we always called 'The Rendezvous', the old brick woolshed at Homebush, always left open for shelter to those who were on the swag.

Yes, this was Kirkman all right even if he did look a stranger sitting up in bed dressed in hospital pyjamas. The goat went off with the local publican after the pubkeeper came to light with some money.

The goat was a great attraction in the hotel yard, but not for long. I can't remember now whether it was the doctor or Kirkman himself who decided the patient was recovered! The hotel keeper rang to ask if the goat was at the hospital? It wasn't and the patient and his mate were well away on the road again, the richer for their holiday.

One day some years back they had called at our neighbours. While Kirkman was talking, the children were vainly trying to catch their mother's attention as she stood at the back door.

"Mum . . ."

"Go away and play! I'm talking!"

"But mum . . ."

"Will you be quiet!"

They went away, not to play, but to watch the goat rapidly strip the rose bushes set out in the new rosebed.

I don't know where the old man ended his days. If it was a dose of brandy and a holiday he wanted when he had his 'heart attack', he deserved it. The cold, the wet, the dusty road, the loneliness, seem in these security-is-everything days to be a high price to pay for freedom and independence.

Hospital nurses, sisters, and doctors from Greymouth to Nelson knew 'Whiskers Blake' (Gregory Henham), one of the last swaggers on the West Coast, recalls Mary Hole of Wakefield and Takaka.

On the quiet, they'd allow him a bed in the Men's Ward if

one was spare on a cold or wet night. But one wintry evening a new doctor curtly showed him the door when he confidently sought a bed in the ward.

Undeterred, the swaggie spotted another big building round the corner, crept up the stairs and into an empty bed, boots and all. He awoke to sharp prods in the ribs. Towering above him was a nurse, plying an umbrella.

"Get out!" she roared. He fled.

We heard later the police station proved more hospitably inclined that night than the hospital, or the nurses' home.

'Whiskers Blake', brought up in Kumara, West Coast, smoked a pipe without a stem, was anti-Catholic, and insisted than when there was snow on Mt Arthur there was fighting in Russia.

Around his 80s, he was seen at intervals trudging along the roads until about 1949. Where he finally halted, who knows?

A swagger who undoubtedly should have been receiving medical attention at times had an extraordinary 'rat test' when he was enjoying (?) himself, to the puzzlement of Mavis Boyd of Foxton:

He wore a dilapidated Army coat, stiff with dirt, and bowyangs on his greasy trousers, and he went by the name of Napoleon: Nap for short.

A scruffy little fellow who followed the shearing gangs that went to the backblocks stations, offering his services as a cook. I wouldn't have liked to eat anything he cooked, but shearers those days didn't have things so good as they do today, and cooks were hard to get.

When the season ended Nap made for a hotel in Timaru, and throwing his cheque over the counter he'd say to the publican: "Here you are boss, tell me when it's cut out," and arming himself with a few bottles of brandy, he'd head for the stables.

He never slept in the hotel, preferring the company of the horses, where he'd settle down with his swag—a dirty old horse blanket lined with old newspapers—and proceed to get gloriously drunk.

If he didn't have red and green rats crawling all over him

he considered that the brandy was no good, and he hadn't got his money's worth.

You'd hear him screaming far into the night as his imaginary rats attacked him. He swore the stable was full of them and he was probably right too.

When they stopped chasing him up the walls—a state of inebriation which he referred to afterwards as 'a jolly good time'—he would pull himself together, roll up his swag, which included a couple of bottles for the road, and hitch a ride back to the open road on one of the wagons which carried bales of wool from the station.

Nobody knew where Nap actually went, but he always turned up year after year, just as scruffy, still clad in the same old Army coat, which seemed to be a part of him for it never wore out.

A Negro swagger Jimmy Green, nationality unknown, had a little girl (now Mrs Hall, born at Mataura in 1889) deeply perplexed. She would follow him discreetly down to the creek, to watch him wash his face.

To her increasing disappointment, none of the black ever washed off . . .

Alice Crosbie of South Westland remembers two swaggers, complete contrasts, calling separately at the farm. One, an elderly cultured gentleman, an old-world courtesy in his bearing, before taking off for a night in the roadman's hut, shared the evening meal, and sat round the family fire for a while, talking:

"He had a mystical turn of mind, words of wisdom and philosophy, new and thought-provoking to us then, just rounding the corner into our twenties, lifting us into realms of mystery and wonder compared with the sometimes dull and prosaic ways of Earth.

"From that day to this, we have never ceased to search and ponder.

"Next day my husband went over to the roadman's hut to see how our friend was managing for breakfast. He came up quietly behind him, as this gentleman (he truly was) was wielding the axe, cutting wood for the open fire. Unaware of my husband standing behind him, he stopped, looked up at the mountains close by, the mists rising, the snow-fed river, and spoke aloud, saying:

" 'How very fortunate I am to have had this night's rest and shelter, to have met that nice young couple who gave me that good meal last night. How lovely is this scene before me! I am a very lucky man. Thank you.'

"My husband turned quietly away, feeling he was intruding."

The other swagger, the complete antithesis, was coarse and hard and brutal, a huge man, unkempt, demanding food, eaten wolfishly. Then a few gruff remarks on 'clink', and the good times he had had there.

"That's where I'm heading back for," he said, in his evil way, standing up and towering over the two, before departing into the night.

Alice herself could "only pray silently that he was not planning to use my young husband and me as a means of getting there."

A few country women, isolated in ways difficult to imagine today, were terrified of swaggers, convinced they were all murderers or thieves. A world of difference lies between loneliness and solitude, but many a woman at times must have been sick and raked with loneliness.

A very small nervous wife with a huge husband with enormous feet always placed a pair of his giant boots outside the front door, and put another pair outside the back door, whenever he was away . . .

"The farm in the valley with its vistas of loneliness," as Alice Crosbie has expressed it.

Resourcefulness, of course, was a game two could play at.

Late one afternoon, writes Kathleen Holden of Alexandra, a strange swagger with a peculiar loping gait came along the road and right into the kitchen, a mad look about him. Kathleen "was transfixed by his funny eyes."

"I want some tucker, missus," he ordered.

Without turning a hair, her mother asked him what he needed. Everything on the shelves, apparently, the pile on the table was growing when mother turned to her small daughter and said casually:

"Kath, it's getting late. Run out and get the chaff ready for the horses, dad will be here anytime now."

"I dashed outside to do a job I had never done in my life, glad to get away from those crazy staring eyes. Within minutes, from the safety of the stable, I saw the swagger scooting round the house and away to the road. Good old mum. Her little ruse had worked."

Entirely different "was a little short man with a rosy complexion a girl could envy," remembers Beatrice Richardson of Stratford.

"His hat sat with a devil-may-care air upon the side of his head. He offered to chop some wood in exchange for a meal, did so, and sat down to enjoy a thoroughly good dinner. He told my goodnatured mother:

" 'Hi 'ave not bin dragged hup,' as he carefully put his cup down inside the saucer and not on the outside.

"Mother seriously assured him that she was sure he had not, as she poured his second cup of tea. She always liked to think the best of them. He bowed when he left with an almost courtly old world air, saying:

" 'Hit's Hangels like yer wot likes to live near 'Eaven, mum—but hits 'ard for sinners to git up 'ere.'

"It was, in fact, a steep climb up the hill to reach our place when a meal was overdue."

On the other hand, angels—or even the good Lord Himself—could pay visits disguised as swaggers, one mother maintained and impressed on her daughter, never turning a tramp away, no matter how scruffy, without a hearty meal.

A swagger calling at a Southland home was given a bible by granny. Some years later this same man called again, and remarked:

"Your mother gave me a bible once. There were some pages missing."

"Did you read what was there?"

He shuffled round evasively, and said:

"She was a good woman, your mother."

Another tramp always asked for a cake of soap, and by the

time he reached a town, he had quite a collection to sell to his buddies—but how many would be interested?

"Oh no! This is too much!"

Mother threw up her hands in dismay (writes Doreen Anne Goss) when she saw old 'Francis' (as we'd nicknamed him after St. Francis of Assisi) coming over our bridge with an aged donkey trailing him—it had been ill and had sore feet, and a circus family passing through intended destroying the poor old thing. Fortunately the old swagger looked after Neddy until his feet got better, and the pair slowly took to the roads together.

But mother, with pressing memories of a weedy but most troublesome piglet he'd saved from starvation and later brought to us, was quite adamant, and after they'd rested overnight, had been fed and given goodies for the pack, she saw them on their way.

Old Francis—he called quite often when he learned we loved and cared for all kinds of creatures at the Thomas's farm, Banks Peninsula, almost 70 years ago—usually had in his coat pocket or within his pack some small creature needing care, comfort, or company.

This swagger, wellknown and well-liked, doing odd jobs round the threshing mills for his tucker, would arrive with anything from a nest of baby fieldmice rescued from the blades of the harvester, to a weka with a broken leg, or a cat with a paw smashed in a rabbit trap's jaws, or a duckling with a leg amputated by an eel in the creek.

Old Francis would usually operate, making splints for the weka, named Hoppy, and a pegleg for the duckling, named Loppy because he walked lopsided, to the irritation of the purebred white Leghorn rooster, the pride of the farmyard. Until he was returned to the bush, Hoppy annoyed mother by stealing shiny bits from the separator drying on a bench near the back door.

He brought us a troubled hedgehog, Hector, who had his own milk dish and liked porridge and buttermilk.

It was wonderful to watch the old man patiently paring the tiny claws of a bird he'd found with a sore inflamed foot—or talking to and calming a bird taken from the jaws of a cat, attending a broken wing. Often the poor little bird was beyond aid, and then old Francis would hold it in his warm hands and in his way comfort it until it died. I've often seen him wipe a tear away.

I like to think of old Francis the swagger in heaven, helping the good Saint of Assisi tend his creatures.

An elderly genteel man, white goatee beard, tall and thin, very shabby, obviously clinging to the last shreds of respectability, chose quite the wrong time to call, seeking a handout at the Esplanade boardinghouse, Wellington, one freezing cold wet winter night around 1930.

His voice caught 13 year old May Donovan's attention "and tugged at my heartstrings.

" 'Have you anything left over, lady, for me to eat?'

"Mum's voice sounded very cross—we were preparing the vegetables for dinner: poor mum, five children and 17 Irish boarders!

" 'Tell him to go away, May—and come in and shut that door—you know how draughty it is round this bench!'

"The old swaggie got the message all right, and much to my astonishment bowed slightly, put up a paper thin transparent hand, and lifted his hat.

"I shivered, tears starting to my eyes, shut the door gently, then rushed out of the kitchen, grabbing on the way three very sour grapefruit (and believe you me, *they were sour*), and by the time the swagger had reached the road again, I was waiting at one of the front windows, thrusting the yellow fruit at him.

" 'Quick! Here ya are.'

"He fumbled as he took them, wonderingly, and then:

" 'God bless you child,' he said in his lovely voice.

"I always felt glad and happy, after someone found him dead in an old shed sometime later, that I did what I could. I've never forgotten his blessing."

"Up swags and away . . .! Come what may . . . No matter how much the cost." That seems the driving force behind many a swagger and his escapades. From Invercargill, J.

Morton wrote to tell how her mother attempted to talk a swagger out of roaming the roads, and instead return to the comforts and security of his well-to-do family:

A wee shrivelled swagman, very withdrawn, known as Scotty, called every harvest time. After tea one night he confided to my parents he was the son of a wealthy businessman.

He said he could not stand the formality and restricted life, so on leaving school ran away, and had never returned. However, after some persuasion he promised he would visit his home and see his mother: he did.

On his next visit to us he said: "Never ask me to do it again, missus. My mother was pleased to see me, but when they showed me into a bedroom, I waited till the house was quiet then crept out, shouldered my swag and off."

No four walls could hold Scotty.

Years later, after cutting a tendon in his wrist and no longer able to cut hedges, he walked over 100 miles to ask my father's help.

After a warm meal, and seated by the fire, he said he'd been offered an old spring cart if he could find a horse and harness. Father hunted for a horse, mother mended warm clothing to fit him out, and we youngsters slipped tobacco and matches into his coat pocket on the quiet because Scotty was very proud. Eventually he set off riding the half-draught, harness strapped around him, his swag of clothes on his back.

He returned once, collecting bottles and rags, still the same little Scotty. We never saw him again.

Our last story in our 'Women Concerned' section I have reserved for J. Banks, of Huntly:

In 1934 I worked as a domestic for a Swiss widow in Pukehou (Hawkes Bay). The same swagger came twice, from whence he came I knew not, but many a time I used to peek behind a curtain, and saw him scratching here and there as if he had fleas.

He used to carry a blackened knocked-about billycan and a dirty grey bundle tied on an old stick over his shoulder, and come to the door to beg for a scrap of bread. My mistress, the good soul she was, would heap up a big plateful of food and half a loaf.

As a servant, I carried this out to the swagger under the trees and would see him wolf down the lot as if his very life depended on it. He left his plate on the doorstep, and as silently as he came he was gone—like a ship that passes on a stormy night. 'Stormy' was his name.

'Anyhow Jesus Wandered Around'

No, they said firmly, they weren't all necessarily 'skin a flea for its hide' mean, these people who refused to give anything to swaggers. Although you feel their attitude would change immediately the tattered boot was on the other foot, they reckoned people shouldn't help scallywagging wayfarers. This only encouraged idle-alongs to keep on roving, instead of making the effort to get regular work 'and settle down'. This belief could have been justified sometimes.

Yet, Stan Knowles wonders, perhaps there's an affinity between the oldtime swaggers and some of the unemployed of our affluent (sic) society: those finding it psychologically impossible to follow out the routine of regular daily work. The irritation of working for another.

"Do you like your new boss?" I asked a journalist.

"I never like *anyone* who's my boss," he replied emphatically.

Prisoners of war, when let loose again after up to four years in captivity, must keep moving about until the 'crowded in' feeling fades. For years later, many ex-prisoners take a wry view of their jobs, once considered so important, and of organised society. They marvel at the prostitution of the word 'freedom' by sheltered, smug, selfish citizens.

"That rotten feeling that *everyone's* your boss," as Frank Tully, a friend who becomes irritated after a while with almost every job, expressed it so well.

Of course if you've got the money to travel, particularly overseas, it's called 'itchy feet', is lauded in beaming advertisements and posters, is said to broaden the mind, and is considered most respectable. Certainly, too, it's magnificent for Youth to see other lands in a world which should have no frontiers, and move as you wish without travelling in great locust-swarms in military uniform. But a few of these 'seeking understanding' are undoubtedly modern swaggers with a mean streak as well, as many a longsuffering peasant must realise!

George Davies of Hastings has an apt word or two on this security-business, helping to place part of the setting and perhaps a little of the unease of the swagger:

I've had a pretty varied career, from goldmining to commercial fisherman-farmer. And I've seen a lot of life in some very odd places, and met some strange people, over my 70 years.

We are all looking for security, but I do not think we will find it in the pursuit of the almighty dollar. The most contented lot of people I ever met were those on the goldfields, drawn together in a tight little community by the slump—and the most discontented were a group of American millionares whom I once had the pleasure of meeting on a bus tour.

I've met some happy-go-easy swaggers too, who would never suffer from hypertension, never land up in the heart units with the little T.V.-monitor-sets on their bedside lockers tracing their hopeful trails day and night . . .

The small farmer to my mind is the salt of the earth, and the whipping boy for every economic juggle that takes place in the markets of the world.

A hint of what one or two swaggers may have felt, (provided hunger and weariness and cold were absent) when the sun went down and a great moon sauntered over the horizon and a hare, mystic, sat watching from a knoll, is indicated by Diana Greensill of the Sounds and New Plymouth:

One of the great delights of a return to living in the open country is a rediscovery of the moon.

In the city the dirty yellow glare of the shadowless streetlights, the restless blaze of the almost-night-long motor traffic, and the gibbering of a hundred neon signs distract the eye and the imagination from the moon's stately orbit.

The country moon is not the moon of the astronauts and the scientists, crater-pocked, dust-covered and more and more littered with discarded ironmongery, but that predictably varying radiance that sails with queenly indifference through the skies—the moon of the ancients, of the poets, of lovers . . . and the restless ones . . .

The lure of the road for one blond-headed part-time swagger in his late thirties, met near Norsewood, and who worked on the Wellington wharf in winter and played in summer, was that it kept him as far away from relations as possible.

"All relations do is cause a lot of trouble."

Marriage? The last thing he wanted was a wife.

"Anyway," he said, "Jesus never married."

"That's entirely different," said his questioner, rather shocked.

He didn't think so. He was leading the same life as Jesus—wandering around.

"These men," summed up a Seaward Downs citizen, "were characters, misfits, and yet had their pride, together with the urge: 'Well boss, thanks. I'll be on the move.'"

For the number travelling the roads, very few caused any anxiety. Some were well educated and enjoyed a keen discussion with the boss after tea—the family could welcome this touch with the outside world, and fragments of countryside doings.

Some were alcoholics, some ne'er-do-wells, some unemployed (a great flood in the bewildered '30s), some remittance men, good or bad, with a zest for life; they wanted to live their lives the way they saw it, rolling stones with plums in their mouths, if the dreadful mutation may be permitted.

All were not dodging work, all were not bottle casualties, the walking wounded of brewery and distillery. Many a worthy citizen, paunchy with possessions, whether he or she realised it or not must have felt irritated at the sight of a swagger turning his negligible back on society and saying so plainly 'Count me out'. A knight in shining armour might have been forgiven, but to be rejected by a scarecrow!

Some were grizzly old devils, some must have stank. Others comment:

"So dependent for a meal and yet fiercely independent and proud. The ones who were not afraid of a hard day's work were a great help to farmers at harvest time."

"Unlike my father, I thought them mostly a bloody nuisance. They used to camp in the woolshed, woolpacks for covering, and go to the cookhouse for a feed whenever it suited them, with no consideration for the cook. According to their reception, on various properties they marked the station gates in code with chalk or bits of soft limestone."

"The times were pretty honest, I'd say. Believe this or not, but many a swagger would leave his swag hanging on a fence on the outskirts of a town—just a sack, rain never hurt it, and it was never interfered with. Safe. Always there when he returned for it."

"I have often wondered what became of these swaggers when their end came. Who arranged for their burial?"

"Mother always gave a swagger a good meal. They usually sat eating in silence on our verandah. Most were uncommunicative and surly and were soon on their way."

"One thing about the swaggers, they always arrived in good time for the evening meal. Two Salvation Army collectors arrived at Hawk Hills well after the evening meal was over, expecting food and shelter. This was provided, but no swagger would put a farmer's wife to this sort of inconvenience."

"In the days of swaggers, country folk went off for a day in town and never thought of locking their houses. It was practically unknown for swaggers to steal anything."

"Almost all swaggers had remarkably good health. Perhaps we all would if we could keep away from bankers, landlords, lawyers, rates, taxes, etc."

"I am sure the majority of swaggers would not envy the old men of today who spend years in palatial homes sitting and waiting for the bugle call. They look so bored, so tired and fed up of what is left of our short journey of life."

> *Were they*
> *the useless dropouts of their day*
> *or were they men*
> *born ahead of their time*
> *determined to enjoy the country*
> *as it was then*
> *and will never be again.*

The swagger, Robert Goodman points out, could be launched on his often arduous career for any one of a number of reasons: he might be fed up with a humdrum job, or simply crave variety; he might be intractable to discipline, or he might have been driven from a settled life by a set-back in a love affair. The possibilities are almost endless.

"But New Zealand's social history has known the swagger by necessity. He was the swagger of the depression years who tramped in search of self-respect, of a life less soul-destroying than the dole queue or weed-chipping on city pavements. Where was he heading for? Did it matter? It was *time*, not distance, that had to be overcome—the months and years until a brighter day dawned for New Zealand and for the world."

They had symbols which they chalked on mail boxes or gate posts—good, indifferent and bad. The farmer known as 'Hungry M' always had an X. O was fair. The 'good boss' mark could have been a tick. A bottle placed in a certain manner by a gateway or an inconspicuous arrangement of small stones was thought to be other clues of what lay within.

An elaborate code of drawn signs or hieroglyphics is supposed to have been used in the U.S.A.—savage dog, police tough, good touch, former prisoner lives here, no money, sky pilot, and so forth—it is much more believable that this was drawn up for academics rather than used in practice on the road.

Many farmers had a doss-house made for swaggers, killing a sheep a week or more for them, partly because of a fellow-feeling, partly through the vague thought that a curt refusal might mean a blazing haystack or shed, gates left open, sheep boxed. One station owner claimed he spent five hundred pounds a years on swaggers. (Would this be an Income Tax deduction?)

A six-weeks swagger 'T.J.' writing in *Fair Play,* January 1894, explained how on the swag he found: (1) Citizens should "remember that generous impulses and warm hearts beat there as well." (2) In April 1893 "The road between Moawhango and Hunterville is the worst, I should imagine, in New Zealand; we were up to our knees in mud and at times could travel no more than at a rate of $1\frac{1}{4}$ miles per hour." (3) The price paid for scrubcutting at Russell's Station, Tuna Nui, "was the munificent sum of 2 5d per acre," the scrub "far from being light." (4) "Life is short. Why not endeavour to make it happier."

A swagger's receptions on Hawkes Bay farms last century are recorded in a diary by the luckless William James Cox, farm labourer and millhand, drain digger and scrubcutter, enduring 45 unfortunate years in New Zealand, born of yeoman stock at Snodshill, Chisledon, England. He set out to walk to Russia (unsuccessfully), and eventually died at 79, of heart failure, at Greytown Hospital, 19 July 1925.

"The two graves—his and Russian Jack's—are at opposite ends of the cemetery, Jack in the newer lawn area, and James Cox's grave is right at the back," reports Matron Pattullo. "I think this area may have been for 'indigent' patients—as they were classified in our old records.

"I have checked an old register and find that James Cox

'Anyhow Jesus Wandered Around' 137

was admitted from Carterton on 15 June 1925 suffering from 'senile decay'. No relative or friend to be notified when he died on 19 July. Poor lonely old man.

"We still have a few. Like one old sailor here who tells us tales of the sailing ships round the Horn and across the Roaring Forties. He ran away to sea when he was about 12 years old, and can't remember about his family."

Cox's swagger-view of various Hawkes Bay stations in the early 1890s is quoted in a thesis by Michael Campbell (1972) from Cox's own 35 diaries in the Alexander Turnbull Library, written in a tiny hand, covering his itinerant life:

> Orua Wharo: "got a good tea but only the bare floor to sleep on."
> Mount Herbert: the Gaisfords gave him bread, potatoes, cold mutton and tea.
> Mangakuri: "a good place to stop . . . two good feeds," but a bad night on a cold floor.
> Elsthorpe: depressing, "the roughest place I ever saw," very "dirty and messed up, the bread stale and sour."
> Te Aute: Parson Williams' station: food good but the whare "infested with rats."
> Poukawa: "some hard biscuits, a very small piece of bread," a "little tea and sugar" and a raw "neck of beef so tough" that it was inedible. This was the "roughest treatment" he'd had.
> Te Mata: "was well treated at Chambers," food good and plentiful.
> Waimarama: no work, but the cook gave him "work for my tucker," 15 weeks.
> Maraekakaho: liked the food but bed "was full of Bugs," swaggers nightly from 5 to 15, estimated from 2,000 to over 5,000 yearly.
> Porangahau and stations down the coast: good treatment.

Maraekakaho Station, says a newspaper reference, ran two cottages for the use of swaggers and as many as a dozen at a time slept there. Each had to get a permit to stay the night and apply at the office for a meal ticket.

In two consecutive weeks, 36 then 42 swaggers called at Greenhills station, Kaikoura, in the bad good old days of July 1880, another miserable depression, when "The workingman able to get neither land nor work had to become a tramp," as Frank Parsons quoted in his *The Story of New Zealand*. He also noted "the uncivilized Maoris" had their own commonly-shared land "so that no one was ever in want."

At Waikakahi, Canterbury, "in the days of Allan McLean's ownership"—say 100 years ago—a building with 16 bunks was for swaggers, and even back in the 1860s, 14 swaggers were at the Levels on one day.

"Hundreds of men in Canterbury and Otago carried swags at some time of the year, in search of seasonal work, as last century neared its end," writes Clem Williams of Oamaru. "My father said that when he was a boy about 1890, while digging potatoes in May by a main road near Timaru, they counted over 110 swaggers passing along the road *in a day!*

"On one harvest-time night, a wellknown farmer had to go to the front gate and turn them away, as his wife had fed about 15 men on top of the harvest workers and was running out of food—and, I would think, patience.

"My father said of 23 young men in Springbrook in 1896 only two had permanent jobs. The rest varied, from casual to the odd one who shot hares and fished, and did practically no work at all. He blamed the finish of the hand-worked gold claim and the decline of railway construction for the surplus of labour.

"As conditions improved some of the men got permanent jobs—the freezing works opened—others took up farms as the big stations were cut up, and only the hard-core working and professional swaggers remained. Even in the '30s a single man could make enough shearing and threshing to live on for the rest of the season, and remember a lot of men stayed single in those days."

Everybody had to carry a swag to get work in the back-country in the old days. You might divide this questing population into three classes—workers going to a job; workers such as the Highland Chief with no home but moving restlessly from job to job; and then the professional swagger who did the absolute minimum. Some had parents or friends where they stayed in the off-season.

When the wheat boom was in its heyday, many of the swaggers provided the mobile work force and the cockies provided huts for them. Swaggers travelling from farm to farm would drop in overnight, using these huts, and often were given food too. When the wheat faded out, goodnatured fellows kept up the old tradition of free shelter and some grub, and were doubly blessed for it during the grinding years of the depression. At less generous and mean places, however, a fair bit of bickering and annoyance arose, with some farmers deliberately burning down the huts to discourage the swaggers from coming their way.

An old Rangitikei house, given over entirely for swaggers to use, went up in flames and no mistake—an astounded Mr Pearce, the owner, from his woolshed on the hill, saw smoke pouring from the old house, followed by a quick exodus of swaggers scurrying off in all directions, no-one waiting for the blame!

A wisp of smoke from under the Kauaeranga bridge with the first cold snap of winter, and sure enough, year after year, old Jack would be found there, in a daze of meth fumes. He would be brought into Thames police station—swag, dangling billy, saucepan, and all.

He always camped under bridges, maintaining:

"You can't beat a meal cooked by the riverbank."

"Six weeks," the magistrate would say resignedly, the maximum possibly then for a country lock-up, and the old swagger would settle in comfortably, pottering about, dozing in the sun, doing a few odd jobs around the station, a languid weeding of the garden, a sporadic sweeping of the cell yard.

His sense of timing was perfect, judiciously gauged so that he appeared to be working whenever the policemen passed through from police station to house for morning and afternoon tea.

Released, ostensibly heading for some small rouseabout job on a nearby farm, within a matter of hours Jack would be discovered passed out, clutching another empty bottle, and the process would be repeated, seeing him warmly accommodated and well fed until September brought spring, the daffodils, and the call of the roads again.

"We had a hut near the house, where a bed was kept ready for the 'gentlemen of the roads'," writes Kathleen Holden from Alexandra.

Near Orua Wharo homestead, Hawkes Bay, drooped a tired old shed known as the Bull Shed, a wellknown meeting-place for up to seven or eight swaggers at a time. They'd taken some sort of fancy to this derelict place. Rather fragile and ineffectual looking arrangements of tin, board and spouting held together with bits of wire nevertheless diverted every drop of rain out of the Bull Shed, where many a yarn was exchanged and many a thirst was well and truly slaked. "No-one was ever turned away without a meal."

Will Trolove, a small-built man who loved his pipe and loved a yarn, had 'The Shades' up past the Clarence River, Marlborough. Swaggers called him 'Captain Kindheart', a good epitaph. He had a hut put up for them across Deadman's Creek. Influenced or not by the name of the creek, they kept the place very clean for the next visitor, without obscenities on the walls, and sometimes a 'Thank you kindly'.

In turn, his son was hospitable to wayfarers.

"They were not all alcoholics or even drunkards," writes Bryan Trolove, describing solitary men of the road.

"But they were lonely characters, leading lonely lives, for unlike their modern counterparts they had no motor cars, no wirelesses, no social halls and no entertainment, and little to spend their wages on except drink."

A few might stay for a while to be cowboy-gardeners if the owner and his wife were tolerant and understanding, and helped to 'dry them out' now and again—Trolove himself was the only mourner at one such old chap's funeral.

They had managed to cure this veteran, a painter by trade, of his habit of drinking methylated spirits and "as a man of experience, he told me that methylated spirit drinkers became a race apart once they'd started drinking this 'lunatic soup' as he called it."

What on earth was drinking methylated spirits like, anyhow? Jack May, a professional swagger in the 1970s and rather proud of his occupation, was heard to remark with a touch of scorn: "Oh no, *he's* not a swagger, he's just a meths drinker."

An old Fong King, after recovering from a bout, told a pal, who told me, these names the initiated call methylated spirits:

> *The Bottle of a Thousand Songs.*
> *Fix Bayonets.*
> *Jessie's Dream* (*I really like that!*).
> *Around the World for Ninepence.*

If a whip-around raised ninepence, the company would adjourn to Hagley Park where the sacred waters of the Avon sufficed for breaking it down, and the national drinking cup was a Capstan tobacco tin.

Brasso and boot polish gave it an added kick. Obnoxious colouring matter could be strained out by filtering tainted spirits through a loaf of bread, a practice also recommended by I'll-soldier-no-more warriors to avoid telltale gunpowder marks around self-inflicted wounds.

The old chap said that on a cold miserable morning after a shot or two you'd be on top of the world, raise your hat to all passing half-frozen strangers, and remark on the glory of the morning.

The blackbirds and thrushes would be flat out on their version of the dawn chorus; any hills or steep inclines ahead of you were mere corrugations—you just flew up them.

The aftermath was hell, poor old chap with his keen sense of humour despite a life of misery.

When they shot him into Cell X and slammed the door, a swarm of brass bees attacked him.

After the police had got rid of that lot and slammed him in again, a great rhinoceros charged him. Talk about

Stanley in Africa: he wasn't in the same street when the rest of the fauna went into action.

Booze certainly sent a lot of footsloggers out onto the roads—but why pick on swaggers this next story seems to ask.

In the winter, when his rheumatics kept him from sleeping out, 'Dad' Kingnan came to town and got a job washing glasses, etc, in one of the local pubs in Wellington, usually The Crown, slept in one of the sheds if they'd let him, and waited for the first signs of spring. Then he'd be away on the road.

"No, I don't read books," he told George Davies who yarned to him during three winters, in the 1930s, and who continues:

"People are my books," Dad went on, "and I meet hundreds on the road, all with different ideas about the same things, and damn few really know where they're going.

"But they make my life—and I can hardly remember getting a surly answer when I gave someone a 'Good Morning'."

An ex-jockey, Dad once rode a horse into a place in the Melbourne Cup (probably then called the Melbourne Stakes), a man who never once spoke harshly of people but simply said, if others were being critical, that people were victims of their own ambitions, and the really happy people were those who were satisfied with little.

Yes . . . a funny little fellow . . . in a black jersey, muffler round his neck, pants too big for him, scuffed shoes, and a little, round, hairy face, twinkling blue eyes, and a peaked cap.

He was much more than a swagger to me; I think he had the answer to that question: "What's it all about?"

"There's nothing quite like meeting blokes on the road," he said, grinning.

"What about eating and living, and all that?" I asked.

The blue eyes twinkled again.

"I work for it," he said. "A bit here, a bit there, I don't need much, *and I never work just for work's sake.*"

He paused, and thought, and then said:

"Tell you what. When you get home tonight, you and mum get a sheet of paper, and write down all the things you could really do without."

He rubbed his face and grinned:

"Course there's always mosquitoes, or bloody sandflies too."

In midsummer, I remembered Dad, his talk of orchards, warm hay, the quiet trout pools, the roadside philosophers. I envied him. He was alive. And me?

I looked at my half empty glass, and remembered he had called it 'The Great Escape'.

"Right. Dead bloody right," I mumbled.

This swagger ('Daddy Kingham', another maintains, pointing out a slight difference in name) stood about five feet four, fairly broad, a stubbly grey beard and blue eyes, dark suit, and brilliant boots: he'd borrow brush and blacking at every opportunity, despite the fact his boots were pathetically full of holes. Jockeys, a close fraternity then, helped him, and he probably had a nest or two round Trentham.

He did the boardinghouses for handouts, and at one, the Esplanade, near the foot of Tinakori road, the father gave him a large parcel wrapped in newspaper. More than 40 years later the daughter of the boardinghouse still finds herself wondering: "When the old chap unwrapped it in some sheltered spot and found a cooked sheep's head, eyes and all, did he remark: 'There's a lot of goodness in a sheep's head'; or did he fling it away contemptuously for the scrouging alleycats, saying: 'Fancy giving a man *that* . . .' "

And, like many swaggers and many old soldiers, Daddy didn't seem to die, but just faded away . . .

Children sometimes really feared swaggers, perhaps through grim warnings from parents, perhaps from their own vivid imaginings as part of a childhood zest in life.

". . . and what would YOU do if he popped you in his big bag?"

"Ooooh, I'd kick and scream and pull out his hair . . ."

Kay Lowen was raised on a fruit and vegetable farm at

Waikiwi, near Invercargill. The road, Bainfield Road, commonly called 'Mud Road' and with every good reason, didn't deter swaggers, and were those children frightened of them? Often they went for their lives, some maybe running still says Kay, some kids howling—all usually very scared of these unknown rovers, always keeping *behind* the swaggers—never passed them, ready to bolt at any moment: "a real tizzy, but we never heard of any doing anything wrong, just wanderers, wanting a free feed. We nicknamed one old bloke Bill Swingleg because of his habit when walking of swinging out one leg then in across the other, a stiff knee, perhaps?"

"When I was very small," notes Mike Henderson, "one winter I found a tramp asleep on the hay in the winch house, Kairuru. This winch house originally was used for hauling up great hunks of white marble to make a memorial where a prime minister's bones lay, Bill Massey, on the left hand side coming into Wellington by sea.

"I think there was snow about. Dad was furious, but mum made the old boy a plate of pickle sandwiches. Can't remember where he ate them, but I think I was scared to eat off that plate again for a while . . ."

Invited into a Takapau kitchen for a meal, this veteran of the roads took his boots off under the table, to the instant reaction and amusement of the children—and there were 13 in the Thomsen family!

Some swaggies appeared only once at a place. Others called regularly—but not too regularly, if they were wise, like family relatives.

Some took a dog with them for company, but more likely, one Southlander believes, to provide a bit of food on days when people were not very generous along the way. Rabbits were plentiful, often a plague, and a hungry dog could be relied on to share his catch with his hungry master. A swagger often asked for salt—possibly to flavour a rabbit stew.

A nippy discreet dog could nab a sauntering straying hen, but many a farmer and shepherd would eye a swagger dog with disfavour, especially about lambing time. (The Far

North had an expression: 'As useless as a gumdigger's dog'.) Such a dog if intelligent would stick close to its master's dusty heels.

A surprise awaited W. Andrew, in the Gisborne-Wairoa area, about 1927 or 1930 "when a swagman told me he was travelling through with Joe Ward, but he had to leave Joe on the outskirts, because he didn't think he'd be allowed in town. He was on the cadge for himself and for Joe.

"Wondering why Joe couldn't do his own cadging, I asked about him—and Joe turned out to be his pet wild pig!

"Of course I took this story with a grain of salt, and satisfied myself that this swagger was a bit touched.

"Next morning, moving off early with horse and gig on my own journey, after a mile or two I saw a swagger ahead of me . . . and walking alongside him was a fully grown ginger-coloured wild pig with no lead, just following on . . ."

And Alice Jones-Sexton of Gisborne quite independently confirms that when she was a pupil at the Makaraka School in 1923, "a swagger with a 'wild-tame' brown pig caused great excitement during the lunch time, and all the children surrounded this unusual couple."

One swagger, a guest round the family fire after having shared tea, looked humiliated when the farmer offered to repair his boots, and did so, but "I shall never forget the expression on that poor man's face when the job was done—thoughts, no doubt, of the weary uncomfortable miles he had walked, and perhaps of a better day to come."

"This misery of boots!" didn't the great H. G. Wells proclaim?

The misery of feet too, most certainly, particularly as the years lengthened, as Jack May knows, and Russian Jack and Barney White Rats knew only too well. Some, around the start of this century, were seen without socks, favouring or using instead strips cut from blankets wrapped round their feet. These were known, perhaps ironically, as Prince Alberts.

Jim Forsyth of Hamilton, in common with hundreds of other New Zealanders seeking work or a bed and a meal, carried the swag in depression days. Forty years later, in Cashel Street, Christchurch, he and a comfortable-looking elderly man exchanged long glances, grinned, wondered where they'd met, then exclaimed simultaneously:

"Hakataramea Valley!"

They'd met previously for an hour or two when both were on the swag:

"We'd boiled the billy together, magged a little about the recent war, and finished up by damning everybody but us two," Jim wrote to me in happiness. "Our meal was the usual bread and butter and a slice of cold roast mutton. I remember too we shared a slab of blackberry pie he had scrounged somewhere. It was heavy and soggy but what cared we of indigestion. It was washed down with that fine brew that can be made only in a blackened battered billy."

Crib over, they strolled to Kurow for a beer, then he made up-river to the high country, Jim headed towards Oamaru.

"Our brief footpath reunion over in Christchurch, I stood and looked after him, stumping sturdily along, short and stocky, head up, shoulders back, and as I looked his clothes changed to sun-bleached blue shirt—sleeves rolled—corduroys caught in bowyangs below the knee—hobnailed boots and an old army lemon-squeezer complete with airholes, and a smoke-blackened pipe."

The companionship of the swag . . .

'The Starlight Boarding House Fraternity'

Stan Knowles's father, who never refused anyone who came to the door asking for food, had no time for any man who claimed to be 'down and out'. He didn't mind swaggers saying they were down; *he just hated to hear any man admit he was out!* More than one swagger received a stern lecture based on this fighting thesis.

Down on his luck if any man was: the very man who wrote our national song, hymn, or whatever, *God Defend New Zealand,* was forced onto the roads, a bitter situation, described by Arthur Vile, now away from The Shiner country and editing a Wairarapa paper.

"Thomas Bracken, author of that classic poem *Not Understood,* former editor of a Dunedin newspaper, and a member of Parliament, had fallen upon evil days.

"He was walking from town to town, selling his poems at sixpence a copy, and when he called upon us, he said that his sales were so small that he could hardly earn enough to buy himself a crust. We had a tarpaulin muster in the office, and raised sufficient to buy him a new pair of boots and pay his train fare to the next town.

"We have seen many sad things in the course of our journalistic career, but nothing sadder than poor Tom Bracken, weary and footsore, trudging from village to village—'not understood'."

Then the goldminer who towards the end of his life was grateful for just a warm snooze. Here's how Don McLennan of Palmerston North met him:

One cold and wet winter's night an old man came into the bakehouse and asked if he could get a bit of a warm.

"Yes," we said.

This man after he had thawed out with the aid of a bit of tucker and a billy of hot tea, entertained us with yarns of the Otago goldfields. He also told us his name was Timothy O'Shea, and that he was related to Les Darcy the Aussie boxer. His yarns about Darcy were true for those of us who were interested in that fighter's career.

The old chap asked us if he could bed down in the stable. We went one better than that, and made a bed for him with empty flour sacks, and laid them under one of the steel ovens, which stood about three feet up from the floor.

Timothy was made comfortable on the flour sacks, and every now and then before he fell asleep, he was heard to say: "Ah this is beautiful, this is lovely!"

That story might bring the suspicion of a tear to the eye of anyone except a land agent.

'Crying Harry', his tears fell like spring rain, but all for a purpose, John A. Lee, whose phrase heads this section, told me over the telephone.

'Crying Harry' would go into a bar and sob so bitterly, maintaining with such conviction that his cruelly-neglected, dear old mother had just died, that even those taken in before grew restless, then uneasy, then guilty, then sympathetic, and offered grog and maybe even a bob or two.

A jovial swagger proved a happy guest for the evening meal, and afterwards performed merrily on the accordion.

"That's great!" applauded Bob, the head of the house, "You'd better come with us to the party tonight and liven it up."

'The Starlight Boarding House Fraternity' 149

"Gee, I'd love to. But look. I've only got my travelling clothes. Can't go to a party like this, worse luck."

"Never mind. We'll find something for you."

And they did, hunting enthusiastically through Bob's wardrobe.

Shaved, spruced up, and neat in borrowed plumes, he enjoyed a really good evening, taking his turn at the accordian to everyone's pleasure.

Next morning, not too early to be sure, Bob went to call his amiable visitor for breakfast.

No swag—no swagger—no party clothes!

Over in Australia, this old swaggie looked a bit done in, so the New Zealand sheepfarmer, holidaying with heart thawed somewhat on the strength of a big wool cheque, stopped his car and offered the sundowner a lift.

The swagman warned he'd no money to pay a fare or contribute to the petrol, writes E. Hill of Korere, but he thankfully accepted the ride.

They sped on, pleasantly enough, until flagged down and booked for speeding. After this they moved at a sedate and rather glum pace until reaching a small town, where the swaggie asked to be put down.

Leaving the car, he apologised again for being unable to pay for the ride, but offered the New Zealander a small black book he had as a token of his thanks—the traffic officer's notebook.

"Jimmy the Rat and Billy the Dog were a couple of hardcase swaggers around Central Otago in the early part of the century, say about 1905," Joe Charles, our country balladmaker, will tell you.

"Dad used to tell how they did a storekeeper out of a bottle of whisky.

"Seems this southern storekeeper used to do a bit of slygrogging, dispensing some local moonshine with the groceries.

"The two swaggers joined the straps off their swags to resemble the reins of a horse's bridle, and one tramp went into the store holding one end and making soothing talk to the 'horse' outside, while his mate out there, holding the other end tight, snorted and stamped in a good imitation of a spirited young horse.

"When Billy the Dog asked for, and received a bottle of whisky after warning the storekeeper that he couldn't leave his newly broken colt, Jimmy the Rat pulled back hard . . . and the rogues scampered off with a free bottle of whisky, well knowing that no slygrogger is going to tell the police he has been robbed like this!

"Then the time two bright lads on the swag got a job cutting gorse hedges in the Methven district, and were told they would be paid up to a distance marked by a cabbage tree. And of course they cut it down and moved it a few chains to their own advantage."

Joe Charles wrote, in his most popular song *Black Billy Tea*:

> *Mouthorgan Jack, and John the Baptist too,*
> *The oldtime swaggers, they knew how to brew . . .*

Incidentally, just how did Joe, who likes his tea weak and without milk, come to write that song?

Helping his neighbour Doug Grey with the shearing at 'Farfield', Joe was told by one of the shearers, Ray Pereka: "When you brew up Joe, none of your dish water! I like my tea black."

"Okay," replied Joe Charles. "Black billy tea it is."

The words stuck in Joe's mind, he told me, the beat of the shearing machines set the rhythm, and *Black Billy Tea* built up, just like that!

"When I get an idea for a song I'm like a hen with an egg," he added in explanation. "I don't know if I do it because I want to, or because I have to!"

A chap arrived at a station at shearing time seemingly too well-dressed to be a swagger, and claimed to be a shearer; there was a spare stand on the board and he was taken on. He was a rough shearer, too many second cuts, and after tea that night the boss came into the hut and told him if he didn't do better next day he was down the road. The man never said a word, but as soon as the boss was out of sight he became very aggressive, and announced to the rest of the hut:

"And a good job the bastard went, I was just going to make a spring."

Swaggers had their little idiosyncrasies, such as Russian Jack with his mutton fat and itches or The Shiner, with his three straw hats worn simultaneously sometimes.

One small oddity about a Canterbury swagger, noticed by R. E. Jacobs, was how, when given a billy of water and a little tea, he "would shake the tealeaves from the paper into the palm of his hand, blow on them, and quickly sort them with a deft finger, and then blowing more than half of them away, remark:

" 'That's all that's any good, missus.' "

Much more alarming, a practice not to be followed if you want to keep on good terms with the lining of your stomach, was the fad of a Southland swagger in the late 1880s or early '90s. He called at the door asking for a cup of tea. Taken inside for his cup of tea at the table, he immediately asked for a lump of washing soda. Obviously he intended to wash his clothes, but no—to everyone's astonishment, he carefully placed the lump of washing soda on the floor, broke it in pieces by tramping on it, dropped one piece into his cup of tea, gathered up the rest and put them in his pocket, and then sat back to enjoy his 'tea and soda'.

"John Burke O'Brien, who wore a top hat and called himself The Honourable, (top hats were abundant in those days) was noted for his habit of attracting attention by having a bath in one of the horse watering troughs which used to be found on many a busy street," writes John A. Lee, sending another story.

"He would strip off, trousers apart, and sit in the trough, wearing his old battered topper.

"He wintered frequently in the Terrace End Jail which the inmates called MacGarvies Hotel after the superintendent."

Some of the ways of the bosses were rather weird, too.

Rupert Morrison, who died with the dreaded 1918 flu,

was a station owner who loved a practical joke. One of his hobbies was to tour the roads in his Rolls Royce and pick up runaway sailors, a lot of them in those days, carrying mostly a small suitcase or just a parcel under an arm. He would take them to his station and put them on a frisky horse, and if they were game to try and stay on, he would give them a few days work.

Catching up with one swagman on the road, he pulled up and called:

"Throw your swag in."

When the swaggie did so, Morrison cleared off, leaving the poor chap stranded and swearing.

About a couple of miles along the road was the Taratahi Hotel. Here the farmer left the swag, together with ten bob.

A new cook arrived at his station. Rupert, the boss, walked into the cookhouse and said:

"Are-you-the-new-and-can-you-cook?" all in one breath.

"If I ain't the best cook you ever had," replied the newcomer, "you can stand me up against the wall and shoot me."

"All right," said the boss. "You get on with lunch, and I'll go and clean the gun."

When the station hands came in for lunch there was no cook, and no lunch, but the boss, learning what had happened, hopped into his car, caught up with the cook, calmed him down, and brought him back, to quit the roads and stay on for a couple of mutually satisfying years.

Picture the plight of the Englishman, not long arrived and not long on the swag, who knocked at the door of a wellknown Masterton farmer and asked for employment during the depression (1930s variety), writes Heather Boyes, Waimiha.

"Know anything about gardening?" the farmer inquired.

"Not much, but I'm willing to learn."

The farmer collected a bundle of cabbage plants and a spade and led the way to the garden patch. "I want all that bit dug," he said, "and then you can plant these. I want them planted leaf down, roots on top. When you've finished, get a meal and bed at the cook house, and I'll come and see tomorrow how you've done."

The Englishman set to, doing as he was told. All the plants went in leaf down, roots up.

That night he worried himself sick, reproaching himself for being a fool planting them that way and wishing he'd done differently.

Next morning the farmer appeared with another bundle of cabbages. The Englishman waited in fear and trembling to be told what a brainless idiot he was as the farmer quietly inspected the garden patch.

Finally: "Well you're the first b . . . . around here to do exactly as you're told, the job's yours, now pull all those plants out and put these in the proper way."

That Englishman I believe worked there for many years.

When E. Turner of Rangiora was a small girl, she knew something was afoot when the boys late from school, came across the paddock with their heads together:

"Sworn to secrecy, I was told they'd just found an old swagger all set to camp for the night in our small empty cottage, used occasionally for casual farm help but forbidden to swaggers because of the danger of fire.

"However, he'd promised the boys something exciting from his swag in exchange for something to eat and a haircut. They were cautiously going in the back way for food and scissors.

"That haircut they gave him certainly would have been with it these days, but then it was a very shaggy cut. Yet the old swagger was happy to be rid of his long crop.

"Then he opened his swag, much larger than the usual swagman's swag. Imagine our surprise when he dragged out a large gangly doll and gave us a fairly good hour's entertainment as a ventriloquist!

"Maybe not Basil Brush standard, but then, in the 1920s, this was the first we'd ever heard, and we thought it just fine."

The family, whose mother stressed swaggers could be angels or the Lord in disguise testing, were about to sit down to tea during the depression when two swaggies called, obviously brothers, so alike they could have been twins, aged about 30, barely 5ft high, with red curly hair. After a meal they were offered a bed.

"Later," goes on W. Warren of Matakohe, "while carrying a pile of dishes I tripped and six dinner plates fanned out. Swiftly the brothers leaned forward and like jugglers, magically caught alternate plates as they fell.

"We children gasped with admiration.

"No further evidence was needed. We were convinced beyond all reasonable doubt that these unexpected guests were indeed visitors from Heaven."

Frail and hungry, this swagger turned up at the back door of the Robert Goodman farm at Piako, wearing a threadbare town suit, broken fancy shoes, and carrying a cardboard suitcase tied with string. Offered a bach, he insisted on lending a hand with the evening milking, and stayed behind to clean up the shed.

Robert, a Frenchman from Paris herself, and with not many years farming in New Zealand, continues in some astonishment:

"When he did come in we were already at table. To our amazement he was wearing a tail coat that looked all the more incongruous for the absence of a collar and tie. Only the top of a singlet showed in the 'V' of the jacket.

"As he sat down I asked him if anything had delayed him. He explained that, as he had only one lot of clothes, he always stripped completely after the evening milking and swabbed them down on the concrete floor with the shed broom. No wonder they were threadbare, I thought.

"Then without our asking for it, we got the explanation for the tailcoat.

"One of the girls asked for the salt. Everard stretched across the table to pass it to her. She reached out for it, but as she took it from his hand it was transformed, miraculously, into a match-box!

"Everard was a stage magician!

"Before the meal was over several more conjuring tricks had baffled us and enlivened the evening. Then, after tea, we were allowed to inspect the innumerable pockets of the wonderful coat from which all sorts of unlikely objects could be produced—including the deep tails themselves, the source of the inevitable live rabbits. Had his last bunny, we wondered privately, been sacrificed to the pot? Before long, to the girls' immense delight, he was drawing a seemingly inexhaustible number of coloured silk scarves from their sleeves and challenging them to find the little silver ball that mysteriously changed places—or so it seemed—under three inverted cups."

An Assyrian 'Pukoury Jack', called twice a year at J. J. Anderson's home at Herbert, south of Oamaru, between 1927 and the '30s.

"While waiting till meal time, he would show us a trick which he called The Disappearing Shilling. He used three pieces of white paper, neatly folded, making three squares each bigger than the other. In the smallest he wrapped a shilling. He turned that over carefully, and wrapped it in the middle sized square of paper and turned that over too. Finally, he wrapped those into the larger square of paper, turned that over and gave it the magical bang with his fist.

"Carefully he unwrapped it, telling us the secret was in the turning of the papers. There in front of us was a halfpenny!"

In Canterbury, one woman displayed with some pride on her mantelpiece some wool and wood-shaving fans, and a jointed wooden doll that danced. These had been left by swaggers, as small presents in return for the usual handouts of potatoes, tea, meat and dripping.

Around the same province strolled Tea-Tree, a debonair swagger swinging one of his carved walking sticks, which he whittled skilfully, always with him until he signed off in an old men's home.

The routine of a swagger dropping in is described by G. J. Nutsford, who carried the swag himself once in particularly hard times, and who found the whole process cruel on his feet, and most humiliating.

Arriving at the sheep station or some other stopping place, the swaggy will dump his swag in a hut or shed provided for him, and report to someone responsible.

There will always be some chores waiting for him—

splitting wood for the winter fires, perhaps digging the home garden, or cleaning out the hen houses—always some job that is not the routine work of the station hands.

These jobs, which he does at his own pace, are his payment for his few days of keep, plus a plug of tobacco, soap, a supply of tea and sugar, perhaps some mending wool, needles and cotton. He will eat with the station hands, who as a rule are glad to see him as he brings news, not of the cities so much but of other farms and country folk.

His short stay over, he goes on his way, perhaps refreshed with a bath, his clothes washed, and with enough meat and bread and tea to keep him till he gets to his next billet. Some would be horrified at the idea of a bath!

Some swagmen were of good birth and well educated—some had skills which brought them a little extra. They seldom fraternised with their own sort. Their beat, their skills and sources of left-off clothing, boots, etc, were guarded jealously.

The Highland Chief (we have no other name) should have a novel written about him, Clem Williams of Oamaru firmly believes. This fading figure has gripped his sympathy and imagination, and he writes (filling in for many another swagger from vanished days as well):

Consider this incident—the scene is the bar of the Kurow Hotel—the Chief has a piper sitting on the bar, playing—both are well supplied with whisky. He has just finished shearing at Haka Station and has a few pounds to spare.

Four teamsters at the other end of the room have had enough bagpipes and make it fairly clear. Finally the Chief rises up and throws the four of them out into the street . . . and then buys another whisky for his piper. The chief is a tall dark man with a dominating personality, not an easy man to live with.

Now imagine—a young man, related to the Chief of the Clan—a proud Highlander brought up to shoot deer and fish for trout. Never learned a trade. Then he leaves home—some trouble?—see the world? Everybody was emigrating.

He comes to New Zealand. There is no place for him—he's not a shepherd—it would be beneath his dignity to walk behind a plough—finally he bows to the need to live, and learns to shear with the blades. A good competent shearer.

Now consider the bar scene. For one day he relives the past. The emotional Gael—he has money—he can drink whisky—he can employ his own piper, and the whisky, the piping and the vivid Celtic imagination carry him back to the days of his youth. The teamsters are just a stupid interruption and at the back of his mind is the bitter realisation that tomorrow or the day after, he will be penniless and on the road to the next station and the next. Never again to regain his old life. Is it any wonder he was a hard, bitter man? And there must have been hundreds like him.

Here now is an indication of the gathering host, and the gathering uneasiness, the bewildered trickle which became a flood, the confusion of those who stoutly maintained "It can't happen here, not in God's Own Country!" when a new lot began taking to the roads, the emerging of the depression swaggers, the unwanted, the unemployed.

One fine sunny morning, the boss came to Ron Webb of Foxton Beach, and his friend Henry, who were working then in the bush in the hills behind Nelson, "and began speaking very humbly with a sort of apologetic tone in his voice." Costs were greater than income, they were 'down the road' and they had to pack their swags. They took the ferry over Cook Strait. Ron writes:

"We had only been on the road for two days when we became painfully aware of what people were talking about when they mentioned the 'depression'.

"At first we met them in ones, and then twos, blokes not too different from ourselves, fleeing to where they didn't know, from what they didn't know. The few we spoke to said they had lost their jobs in the slump. Then they started coming more frequently in twos and threes and in parties of three or four, and one or two even had women with 'em, and a couple of parties, it grieves me to say, as a bushman, even toted suitcases.

"I noticed Henry's brows coming down in increasing displeasure and amazement. The numbers grew the further we headed north. To me it began to get a bit frightening.

"The last straw came one day, as far as my companion Henry was concerned, at the sight of a bloke carrying a billy in one hand and a violin in the other. We retired to the side of the road and boiled a billy of tea, as if the last sight had been too much for both of us. Henry remained silent for a long while, which was most unusual for him. Eventually:

" 'I think I know the very place,' he said. 'The prettiest and neatest Maori village you ever set eyes on.' "

Tactics could be important, remembers Molly Vallance of Napier, who had her last encounter with a swagger in 1970:

A tiny, elderly man (she relates), clean and warmly clad, so bright and perky.

"Could you give me some boiling water, missus?"

He handed me a billy, well smoke-blackened on the outside, but scoured to shining brightness inside.

"Can you throw in a handful of tea, missus?" Then, "I wouldn't mind a drop of milk and a bit of sugar, missus."

"Okay," I answered.

The water was almost boiling when he called out again:

"Hey missus! Could you spare a slice of bread, and a bit of butter, and a bit of meat too missus?"

I chuckled as I scouted around for a small bottle of milk, and a jar of sugar. I popped a loaf of bread and a half pound of butter into a bag. "No meat," I apologised, adding a good sized lump of cheese to his parcel.

He beamed as he accepted his lunch: "Thanks, missus. Bless you, missus."

I wonder where he is now. He was such a tiny, little old man.

A specialist in avoiding any hint of work was Jack the Bear, who always had a grouse, particularly against the government of the day, writes Allister Evans, raised in the wide open spaces near Timaru.

Jack the Bear always stood at the back door, or close by as he waited for his meal and his billy of tea:

"All over the Mackenzie Country I've been. Work is 'ard to get these 'ere days. The government's rotten. Half the country will be unemployed."

He always wore an old hat, and smoked one of those large U-shaped pipes.

"Everyone should smoke. It kills the germs and . . ."

"There aren't any germs out here in the country air!"

"The country's rotten. If the government would only DO something, there'd be no unemployed."

"Would you really like a job?"

"Sure, missus, I would."

"The chaffcutter's coming tomorrow morning. Help fork on the stack?"

"Or-r-r no, missus. On the Public Works I hurt me arm."

"Help at the bag-hole and sew up the bags—easy work."

"Or-r-r no, missus. Hands hurt at the war, me fingers all stiff."

"Drive the water cart—get water?"

"Or-r-r no, missus, I hurt me back when a boy, see?"

Mother gave him his lunch and billy of tea, but for once Jack the Bear didn't ask to sleep in the barn. The offer of work, and the chaffcutter arriving next morning were too much for him!

He threw his swag over his shoulders, set off down the road at a brisk walk, and never stopped till he rounded the Lime-kiln Corner over a mile away!

Dags

Hawkers and—well—unusual characters who could move about a bit, who chafed at suburban roots, these weren't swaggers, but some kinship of restlessness was there.

Sort of keas in the land of the kiwi, which is a dull, predictable, myopic bird, distinctive only in what he can't do, and not much of a national emblem.

Hooray for the kea, kidney fat and all, and he and she won't live in the North Island either . . . hmm . . .

During this work, some dags bobbed up (if you know of any, please send along to be part of Book Two, why shouldn't they be recorded anyhow?) and here they are, in a little huddle of their own, keas—or weird old culls refusing to go through the race.

"Like a young colt," at the age of 70—that's how the Dunedin-born newspaper owner with 70 years in New Zealand journalism, William Hearn Thomas of Taumarunui, described the vigorous and rare Jack Allen of the King Country. Here's how Jack, an outdoors man who probably would be furious if compared with a swagger, appeared to William in his memories called *The Inky Way:*

He was over 70 years of age and boasted that he could do most things from shooting to climbing rugged mountain tracks better than any other man of his age in the King Country. For a wager, in Australia, he had driven a flock of geese from Melbourne to Sydney and, for another wager, while living in the Taumarunui district, he climbed to the top of Mt Egmont barefooted within a certain time limit.

Even at 70 years of age Jack Allen was a champion shot with a gun, whether hunting game for his own use or taking part in pigeon-shooting championship events. He won the championship at Stratford one year by killing 13 birds out of 14.

The old man believed in living the simple life and slept out in the bush with no covering but a couple of rugs in the dry fern. Whether in country town or the metropolis Allen could be seen bareheaded, with flowing white locks and bushy white whiskers—like a young colt in perfect health as the result of his open air life.

There was a time when Jack Allen went to Auckland and created a mild sensation as he walked down Queen Street in his everyday rig—shirt and trousers only—with bare chest, bare feet, and flowing white mane.

"White curly locks and white beard rearing up in the frosty scrub—we kids would get a hangava fright, but it was only Jack Allen, swagger of the King Country," writes Charles Whiting of Naenae. "His oddity was he never wore a coat or jacket, always in rolled-up shirtsleeves, waiting for the man who stole his wife. He wore no socks either, and came originally from Australia.

"Jack would doss down in bush huts, sheds, haystacks, or the open. He carried a black billy and a small sugarbag. Now and again he'd swipe a harmless bit of fruit from an orchard and sell it, and tried hawking some fish—but they always went bad on him!"

N. F. Wheeler of Taumarunui and his small sister back

around 1932 were approaching Ohakune Junction station about dusk "when a scantily clad barefooted man with long white hair and beard popped out of the shadows and exclaimed loudly: 'BOO!' We broke all records to reach the friendly lights—Jack Allen!"

Usually remembered as "tall, strong, this handsome and healthy man of the outdoors," Jack is seen as a pink streaker by Veronica Haughey of Wellington, who writes:

Taumarunui Railway Station always recalls to me the rather bizarre figure of Jack Allen, thin and wiry, a mop of white curly hair, barefooted, carrying a gun, rather raggedy white drill trousers and white shirt . . . many people of the King Country-Tauranga area must have tales of him.

People used to ask him for weather predictions (some thought him an expert here), he came and went silently, sometimes lending a hand with some slight job, apparently needing no help himself. Did he have some Aborigine blood? Certainly he liked to 'go walkabout'.

In a borrowed pair of long pink combinations, his white hair tied up in a pink ribbon, riding a white horse without a saddle, I saw Jack Allen enter for a race in the gymkhana at Taumarunui recreation grounds.

Win or not, I do remember he stole the show!

On Taumarunui Station, I've heard, about 1940, as an old man in his seventies Jack took ill, was taken to the hospital up on the hill, and had a comfortable end with kind people in attendance.

I was glad to learn Jack Allen's life of wandering closed like this, and that he was not alone, as he could have been in some out-of-the-way bush hut.

A nurse knew of this end, Helen F. Graham of Otorohanga, recalling "the time he came to the hospital on the hill, with all his possessions.

"But his spirit could not be confined in those four walls, and was so very soon away to the winds, the sky, the natural elements he knew so well.

"Poor old Jack . . . I wonder who came to mourn his passing?

"Among his things, which were handed to a bewildered

nurse to enter in the Property Book, was a deerskin, which served as his groundsheet, as part of his bedding.

"I was transferred from that ward at the time and when I think of Jack, I still wonder idly: What did happen to that deerskin?"

When the Big Brother national computer begins to hum, listen for ghostly chuckles from two Wanganui characters, Shamrock and Granny Dalton, appearing here thanks to the Wanganui Public Library and A. L. Kirk, who wrote:

Shamrock was born John Horsley. He came into prominence in Wanganui first as a shoe shine boy and then as a hawker of fish. He would buy his fish off the fishing boats at the town wharf. Pushing his barrow up Victoria Avenue to the Rutland Hotel corner, his cry of "Fish Fish, Alive Alive O!" was wellknown. After selling a fish he would spend the proceeds in the bar. If he sold too many fish it was not long before he was drunk. Although the police were tolerant of Shamrock, the time would come when he had to be arrested and he would be up before the Court next morning on a charge of being drunk and disorderly.

Some of the larrikins of the town used to delight in stealing his barrow. Shamrock would go to the police station and report his loss and leave it to the police to restore it to him.

He lived at Putiki, and residents reported his whare was spic and span and as any woman would have kept it.

Shamrock was a public spirited man. On New Year's Eve he invariably led the Pipe Band on its march down Victoria Avenue. The Band would not start until Shamrock, dressed in his Admiral of the Fleet uniform, appeared and took his place at the head of the Band.

In 1934 during the depth of the depression, a carnival was held, beginning with a procession, and Shamrock led it.

However, Shamrock earned a great deal of money for the carnival with his impersonation of the Wild Man from Borneo. He was placed in a pit and given shin bones of raw meat with which he gave a most realistic display. Many a child left the tent completely terrified by his performance.

In 1939 he went home to England where he stayed two

years. However, as his obituary recorded, "The call of New Zealand remained strong within him, and he returned to where the lapping waters of the Wanganui were as music to his ears."

He collapsed one day in 1945 and was taken to Wanganui Public Hospital where he died next day. With his death, Wanganui lost one of its most colourful characters.

Granny Dalton, the old Irishwoman, could be seen walking round the town, usually accompanied by her companions, some geese, a cat and a goat. Most unprepossessing in her appearance, she was minus many teeth, and always she smoked a short clay pipe.

It is not known where or when she was born, or whether she was married, but she had at least one friend in a well-dressed woman from New Plymouth who occasionally visited her. Speculation at the time had it that the woman was one of two children whom Granny Dalton accompanied to New Zealand—either as a guardian or godmother.

Granny originally lived in an old shack where Queen's Park is now, then at the end of Taupo Quay, until she built a shanty near the present hospital. Unfortunately it was burned down and Granny lost the few possessions she had. After this, the Police placed this independent old woman in the Old People's Home but she resented the regimentation and walked out.

She took refuge in the scrub at the corner of Purnell and London Streets. A track leading from Parsons Street to the corner became known as Granny Dalton's Lane. Here the late Tom Bristol befriended her. The Collegiate boys built her a substantial cabin. However she was still a frequent visitor to town with her sack on her back. Her 'God Bless You's' in Irish brogue, accompanied any gift of food for her or for her pets. She died about 1905.

Early Oamaru surely must have had more colourful characters than any other town of its size in New Zealand, wrote our valued recorder and horse artist Violet Kerr, describing Trotter Bob in her last letter a day or two before her sudden death in August, 1975. Violet, with her eye for the human comedy and quirks, continued:

Dunedin may have been responsible for some of the odd types who drifted into Oamaru. Before Christmas each year, Dunedin, with true Presbyterian zeal, had weeded out undesirable characters who might have caused disturbance during the festive season, and sent them on their way. They usually headed north. While Dunedin's Christmas may have been more respectable and sober, Oamaru's was certainly merrier.

Bob Harvey was a wellknown Oamaru figure in the 80s.

He hawked pigs' trotters and tripe around town, but mostly had his stand near the old railway station. He had a special cry of:

Fresh pigs' trotters and tripe, tripe tripe!

which cheeky small boys imitated, much to Trotter Bob's fury. He was said to be a very bad tempered and morose man, and it was rumoured that he was titled—but Bob never spoke of his past.

Apparently at one stage the trotter business hadn't been flourishing, for Bob became well behind with his rent payments. His landlord, failing to get any money out of him, finally got rid of him by removing several sheets of roofing iron from the region above Bob's room.

Latterly, Bob Harvey lived alone in a cottage on Cape Wanbrow.

When hawking his trotters, he usually wore a long dress-coat and a top hat. He was short in stature, with long sandy whiskers.

He died in the Tyne Street Old Men's Home in the late 90s.

John the Baptist (could our Canterbury character later have been named as some sort of successor?) was wellknown in the late '70s. He was either part-Negro or Indian, and hawked frost-fish around Oamaru and, also like Trotter Bob, near the Oamaru railway station. During winter John would begin his search for these fish, shortly after midnight, tramping the seashore sometimes as far south as Moeraki, usually lightly clad and often in freezing temperatures. A friend, Sam Larkins, would row him across the Kakanui river. After a good night's collection, he would return to Oamaru loaded down with the fish hanging round him.

Milling and roistering with other dags in our fond *History of North Otago from 1853,* are Cranky Kelly flourishing his green flag, Oyster Ben, Dancing Alice, the redcoat with his bell, Spring Heeled Jack, The Right Honourable Sir (?) John Burke O'Brien (charmingly spoken, insisting he was the first inmate of Dunedin's new jail, claiming to "have been in all the hospitals of New Zealand with diseases, external and internal . . . cured with my own humble prescription brandy and milk, twenty-four times a day," dying in an Auckland inebriates home in the 1920s); Turnell the Mimic (gobbling like a turkey when pompous patrons took their seats at a theatre show)—and, for good measure, little stories and details such as how, to the joy of Oamaru onlookers, drooping decaying cabhorses reared, leaped and fled when circus elephants trundled onto the scene.

In windy Wellington, where the twin dragons Evasion and Delay roar overhead, where career chameleons sit behind glass and smile, Sid the Bottle Oh plied his useful trade.

Sid hauled his barrow around suburban streets in pre-World War Two days collecting empty bottles and other trifles, bowler hatted, multi-waistcoated (goodness knows how many!), plus coats and mufflers draped about his sparse frame, even as the gharry drivers of Cairo.

"But," points out Charles Dennistoun-Wood, "if you were a Sunday afternoon visitor to the Wellington Public Hospital, you saw a remarkably transformed Sid—a Sid shaven and neat in 'Sunday best' blue suit. He sat beside and chatted with any patient who had no visitor, invariably leaving some small and kindly gift.

"Then those two negroes working on Wellington's wharves, one of them revealing his flashing grin, not of white teeth, but amazingly, a complete set of gold teeth. The other was an underwater swimmer extraordinary, and by night a patron of the concert halls.

"His visiting card proclaimed him a Professor of Underwater Swimming, and carried a string of initials following his name denoting undoubtedly self-bestowed diplomas. But certainly nobody could deny his prowess in the water, as any lunchtime bather in the old Te Aro baths could testify.

"But really it was in the theatre that the Professor came into his own. Opera, piano recitals, orchestral performances—he would almost certainly be there, immaculate in full evening dress and a scarlet lined cape. His servant, also a negro, accompanied him into the theatre carrying the great one's opera hat and the musical score. Their entrance and majestic walk along the centre aisle to two of the best seats in the Town Hall was something to which theatregoers always looked forward.

"He eventually left Wellington for Hawaii. The place was never quite the same again."

Now picture the hawkers, swarthy, moustached, darting like famished fowls at fragments of the English language, with packs on backs, or with a burdened horse, or horse-pulled van, making their rounds of the countryside. Those vans opened into caves of wonder for children peeping wide-eyed in the back, wonderful colours with fabrics and clothes, shimmering dressing-gowns from the East, scarves from India, tablecloths, gaudy satin cushion covers, ribbons and threads.

Sometimes a runaway sailor appeared at the back door, displaying with the air of a fellow-conspirator, silks for sale. Usually these callers were Syrians, or 'Afghans', from North West India rather than from Afghanistan.

A mobile draper touring Nelson Province with van and horse was Jimmy Baracat, who also made a far-from-vintage wine at Riwaka, between the river and the foot of the hill.

Jimmy, hawking an assortment of clothing over from Nelson to the West Coast in the late 1920s, always stayed a night at the Motupiko Hotel. One night, when the publican's wife brought in from outside a great armful of wood to fling on the diningroom fire, "from the wood came a whiff of that very strong, nasty smell wellknown to all New Zealanders," relates Mary Hole.

" 'These black beetles smell terrible, don't they?' she remarked conversationally to the guests assembled round the fireplace.

"Jimmy furiously retorted:

" 'Black beeples don't smell any worse than white beeples do!' "

Ahadibox Mulloch, affectionately known as 'Hatbox', a lightly-built Indian of medium height, is still remembered in the St Bathans area which was part of his circuit. The sides of his horsedrawn van folded out to reveal in pigeonholes clothing, towels, materials, and small gifts such as pens. He slept in a sort of narrow passageway in the middle, between the pigeonholes.

Hatbox, very kind to his two plump and shining horses, told an impatient waggoner around 1905:

"You whip my horses I cry."

Sitting by the fire at the halfway house in the Cromwell Gorge (a place used by waggoners) Hatbox told the company he was religious, and didn't like to hear people swearing, Ernie Ball remembers, describing the Indian as "a good joker, but the larrakins teased him too much."

Next morning, going to the front door, Hatbox saw his two horses disappearing round a bend on the main road. The waggoners had let them out. Hatbox turned to the landlady and spluttered:

"Go inside good lady I b....y soon swear now!"

(Here we must record 'Jimmy the Grunter', neither hawker nor swagger, but a character and a pretty solid drinker. Down at St Bathans where frosts could be a good 32 degrees and it really freezes, one cold night he got cast and lay in a pool of water on the road. His longish hair got frozen to the ice, helpers had to cut it off to move him, *and they reckon he never stopped grunting ever after.*)

Mrs Bakus, perhaps a Greek, pushed a large baby's pram with over-large tyres, packed with three or more big suitcases full of trinkets of all shapes and sizes. She took the lot by train part of the way, then literally 'shoved off'. Big, strong, middleaged, Mrs Bakus must have walked a massive mileage all over Otago Central.

Rather than the expense of a hotel, many hawkers preferred to take a very small tent of their own and pitch it out of the wind, quite comfortable with experience.

John Shaw, from England and Australia, was known over Canterbury, displaying from his packhorse crockery and household goods, and also buying horsehair, a good market for this in those days for such things as upholstery and mattresses.

A father and son Afghan-type sold oddments in demand on out-of-the-way stations and little farms—working shirts, thick socks, silk and wool stockings, butterfly brooches, aprons, dresslengths, great pendulum boots for hobnailing and scaling back-paddock Everests, slick shoes for the city visit and dance hall or uneasy church services in the owner's sitting-room. Pipes. And dashing pocket hankerchiefs too, such as the ones Herbert Sewell of North Canterbury examined with interest, "with a horse shoe in the centre to bring you good luck."

Those crisp white folded fake handerchiefs immaculately arranged in a jacket pocket—two peaks at the top, and stapled into a double fold of cardboard at the bottom!

Herbert Sewell said these hawkers got their goods from Dunedin, from a merchant-importer named Soloman George, a Syrian who would rail goods and orders to particular places as the hawkers moved about—a steady trade in working clothes and cheap suits, and stuff suitable for country stations.

Here is a story carried on the wind some nights—told by H. J. Kavanagh, in Bryndwr:

Gypsies in New Zealand! In caravans, on the move, or encamped by the roadside in true Romany fashion! I have a vivid recollection of a particular group which arrived regularly at a spot opposite Louis Crequer's place in

Gilberthorpes Road, Hornby, tethered their well-groomed little pony in the lush grass and, after a few days of peaceful seclusion, moved on.

They were a superior class of gypsy. That was evident in their deportment, their industry, which was of an artistic nature, and most of all in the ornate quality of their caravan which, spick and span inside and out, was a really exquisite piece of carriage building.

A stock witticism of journalists of small town newspapers was to report that 'Three swaggers passed through here yesterday. Nothing missing.' After the outbreak of war in 1914 this troupe of gypsies did not reappear, and as far as I was concerned, there *was* something missing.

Suspicion of gypsies is age old; and suspicion of aliens has never run higher in New Zealand than it did then. They could not have been insensitive to it—and so my gypsies must have departed these shores. Whither?

Did they take their caravan and their well-groomed little pony . . .?

'The Tallyman', as Taranaki people called Pete, the old hawker round Stratford district, slept in his cart and considerately had "a kind of well" built on the bottom, where his shaggy cattle-dog Ben could sleep on wintry nights.

Ann Bradley remembers especially hatpins, an occasional wonderful and most improbable French perfume, and the reek of his garlic sausage, munched with bacon, mushrooms or eggs fried over his evening fire. Often food would be bartered for goods—say, bacon for blankets.

"He never kept books, but if not paid on the spot he would chalk the debt up on a wall inside the customer's house. The lettering was curiously like the broken English he spoke. Everybody could see this, and woe betide any youngster who thought of trying to rub it out. The child would get the mother and father of a telling off, and threats of what Pete would do to him."

The old hawker died on the job, in the dark, his dog lying across his body, guarding him angrily against allcomers, until he was shot, as his master had to be moved.

"The old man's name had a lot of z's and k's in it . . . no relatives were traced. That's how the Tallyman came to be put in father's plot in the local cemetery.

"As father said: 'How could one do less for a friend?'"

'She Could Have Nearly Howled'

Break your heart, that photograph of Barney White Rats, mercifully preserved and kept by R. Little of Oamaru. There's a picture of New Zealand for you—an old tottering swagger literally on his last legs . . . bent, shrunken and blurred . . . stick and dwindled swag—surely even the doughiest reader can *feel* his sore old feet.

'Professor' Barney Winter, or just Barney Winter, or Barney Wasserbrunner, and his performing white mice (not rats) and shadow-shows he'd give schoolchildren for a penny, sometimes threepence, adults sixpence. He always let the youngsters know in advance, so they'd have the money ready. His shadow-show on his back, his own shadow-show faint and nearly completely faded and forgotten for our history.

What are shadow-shows? A primitive pre-movies kind of entertainment with shadows from hands and cut-outs or marionettes thrown onto a white sheet. The light, behind or to the side of the operator, would be from a box containing candles or a lamp.

"Remember it would be pretty low grade projection by today's standards," points out Clem Williams, after experimenting with candles to duplicate a shadow-show. "I saw

'She Could Have Nearly Howled' 173

Magic Lantern slides in my boyhood. It's not likely Barney carried a lantern with him, and there would be the cost and bother of buying kerosene. I would guess he used a candle and some form of box to concentrate the light."

Barney White Rats was swagging between Middlemarch and Palmerston, and he'd arranged to show his performing mice at the Moonlight School, the social centre for such performances then, before 1900. He also bred his clever mice and sold them for 2/6d each.

Barney, (my father would continue,) wrote William K. Roy from Balclutha, was picked up and given a ride by a farmer from Moonlight called Kneebone. Thankful for the ride, the old swagger told the farmer he and his family could see the performing pets that night free—just say they were the Kneebones at the door.

Mr Kneebone told everyone about giving Barney White Rats a lift in his cart, and the free pass on mentioning Kneebone.

They reckon all you heard at the door that night was "Kneebones, Kneebones, Kneebones," until Barney realised he was being taken down, and shouted loud and clear: "Kneebone, Hambone, or Shinbone! There are no more of your Bones getting in here without paying!"

"Barney was supposed to have been a big man in circus circles in the United States in his younger days, but my earliest memory of him was of a short wizened fellow who seemed to be down on his luck. He used to claim that he had given a command performance before Royalty. If that be true, his entertainments at public schools with his white mice at a 'penny a pop' is but another instance of 'How are the mighty fallen'."

So writes 'an old resident' in the excellent *History of North Otago from 1853,* a paperback from the *Oamaru Mail,* continuing:

"However, he provided a laugh for the schoolboys in the old school in Greta street close on 60 years ago," [since 1880] "and there was scarcely a school throughout the district 40 years ago that had not been honoured at one time or another by this queer relic of the sawdust ring."

Another oldtimer, George White, told how Barney wandered into a N.Z. Loan & Mercantile Agency Company auction sale, calling:

"Mr Burbury! Can I have a bid?"

"Certainly, Barney, what's your bid?"

"I bid you good morning," and away he toddled.

Clem Williams's mother remembered him coming to the Otipua School about 1895. He must have given advance notice of the show, because everyone had 2d each. She said he was finally barred from the schools as he got older and dirtier.

When he, or she, was a small child, 'Southerner' of Wairoa saw "The Shiner and Barney White Rats, true 'knights of the road', who roamed through South Canterbury and Otago in the years 1895-1920:

"Barney White Rats was a little, shrivelled-up man with a small whisker. His clothes were very much too large; his trouser legs trailed in the dust, the tails of his tattered coat flapped low behind his knees, and his sleeves hung down to his finger-tips. He received his name from his custom of visiting the various schools to give entertainments, the chief attraction of which were his performing white mice and his amusing shadow-shows."

"He would draw a big crowd and be a sensation. For many years he gave one-man vaudeville shows in and around the Otago gold-mining town St Bathans," wrote G. M. Garrett, a historian interested particularly in the *human* past, in the *Central Otago News* of 2 February, 1965. "He was a remarkable character. He could sing, was a good ventriloquist, and carried a box almost as big as himself.

"This box contained his magic lantern, his screen, the marionettes, and the performing white mice. His marionettes of ducks and geese were very popular, as he caused them to swim across the screen as the highlight of his show.

"This was the first introduction of 'movie-pictures' in Central Otago.

"The children adored him and followed and watched him. They imitated his talk, his walk, and his songs. He had them behind him as the Pied Piper had rats, and when he gathered up his swag and stepped onto the road, they watched him out of sight.

"He was their wonder. Alas, these 'marvels' now would go unnoticed."

Before visiting St Bathans, Barney called at least annually at the Hawkdun station, run by Mr Burnett, later mayor of Dunedin. By certain excuses, such as losing or mislaying essential equipment, Barney usually managed to extend his periods of free board and lodging to about a week, Mr Burnett casting a blind eye on Barney's subterfuge.

"In response to a notice written on the St Bathans school blackboard, my elder sister and I, about 70 years ago trudged some one and a-half miles one night to see Barney's show," writes Ray Jewiss, now of Howick. "We were rather late, or perhaps Barney's perpetual thirst prompted him to get going early, but before our entertainer had recited the last few words of his show, to our great surprise the ducks and the geese all appeared to swim over Barney, the candles and the models of these birds were all bowled over, and Barney too.

"What a hullabaloo! The culprit, quite unconnected with the performance, was a lad of about 14 years. He'd delivered the fowl blow, which had disrupted the show, with a pillowcase containing feathers or chaff.

"Loud protests came from the audience, particularly from the young wielder of the pillowcase who was assuming innocence and threatening others with what he would do to them if poor old Barney was subjected to further violence.

"The sportive youngster then rearranged the apparatus, and a further collection was made and presented to Barney. Repeating his performance a couple of times, Barney packed up his gear and hastened to the Vulcan Hotel to quench his thirst."

Barney must have become resigned to occasional buffeting, this "smallish man with a greasy suit and hat and grey whiskers," as Dick Thomas of Oamaru saw him when a small schoolboy at Otekaieke over half a century ago.

"Barney, receiving free meals from us and from others, usually slept under the northern abutment of the Otekaieke rail bridge, and many of us, I regret to say, threw stones at him."

"The quaint old figure of Barney with his pack approaching the old schoolhouse was the signal for joy at the prospect of stowing away school books and slates for an afternoon's entertainment," writes Bernard Magee in *The Otago Daily Times* in 1952. This was better fun than a trip to the pictures with ice cream and sweets for a later generation.

Small, with ragged concertina-like trousers, his well-worn boots seemingly heel-less, a large coat and bun (bowler) hat, "Barney carried a staff nearly up to his shoulder and a large pack weighed the little fellow down. He had a shuffling gait and looked as if he had stepped out of the pages of a Charles Dickens story. [Some claimed] he was one of the originals of Dickens's two characters in *The Old Curiosity Shop,* Codlin and Short.

"Winter was a showman in London before sailing for New Zealand," goes on Magee.

"In January 1849 Robert Winter arrived in New Zealand as an able seaman on board the sailing ship *Mariner*. He deserted the vessel at Port Chalmers and then began his long life of entertaining the schoolchildren all over Otago and Southland, and at times further afield.

"Winter's first essay at entertainment was the old-time 'Punch and Judy' show, commenced in London and carried on in New Zealand. But Barney was versatile and able to gauge public preferences and aversions in the field of entertainment. Later, he turned to the monkey and organ to enliven the drab days of outback settlements and schools. This in time yielded place to trained white rats (sic), from which his cognomen 'Barney White Rats' originated."

Among those youngsters entralled in his audiences were two small girls, who would write about him 70 to 80 years later. One we keep to use a page or two later as a sort of little epitaph on Barney; here's the other fan of long ago:

"I'm 84," writes Mrs Henrietta Jane Hooper of Oamaru, "and when I was a child I can really remember Old Barney, as we kids called him. It came about like this. My dad, no matter who was swagging on the way, always picked them up, and always a meal and a room off the horse stable, where a a bunk was, and they slept there.

"Barney was a frequent visitor at Moeraki and of course always gave the children a night's entertainment for 3d. each.

"You ask about his shadow-shows, and what they were.

"He would rig up a dark rug three parts up the open door in the school and have the top part set off in white calico. He had six white mice that performed, and a makeshift bridge rigged up on the white part. Barney sang to moving figures worked by wires, singing (and not a bad tune, either):

> *The bridge is broke and I've come to mend it,*
> *Fal dal de diddle all the day*

"Then he'd make the mice perform, sit on their hind legs and wash their faces, and do tricks all much to the amusement of we children.

"He always had many extra clothes on him, far too big, but an honest chap who walked the country."

Gilbert Nisbet, 92, of Weston, who has worked and lived in this district all his life, in a special recording made by Robyn Farrant for our book, told his son Bert, aged 57:

"I knew him and I saw his show. In those days we called it a peep show. He came to Totara School where I was a pupil and asked the master if he could put on his show next day, at 4.00 pm, and admission was threepence.

"Between the porch and the classroom was a door. He tacked a blanket across and above and also tacked up a thin white screen. It looked like cheesecloth, and across the screen he placed a bridge cut out of thick cardboard, and when the performance started a swan appeared, as if it was swimming, its long neck going up and down in the water. Then appeared the form of a man with a gun and by this time Barney had this man saying he was going to shoot the swan. The man took aim and fired and the swan sank out of sight. That was the end of the show.

"He used both hands, one for the swan and one for the man. The shot that was fired was a small red cracker, and at the side of the screen he had a candle alight that helped throw the image onto the screen and also to light the cracker. When he took his blanket down, we went through the door and that was when I saw the cracker and the cardboard bridge and the candle."

"This Barney White Rats—any idea of his nationality?"
"Well, he was more like a Hindu. He was a very small man above five feet and he had a sort of stoop. He was very bandy in the legs, pigeon toed, his clothes hanging on him because they were many sizes too big for him. He had an enormous big nose (hooked) and was very dark skinned with his skin pulled over the bones whiskers, and I never saw him with his hat off. He had an old bun hat and the bun was that large, and he had enormous big ears and when he pushed the bun down his ears stuck out like an elephant.
"He was a real freak to look at. It was not a swag that he carried on one shoulder like the ordinary swagger, but a box."

"Was he a swagger, or was he just a man on the swag?"
"He was actually a swagger. It was a box with a blanket wrapped around it. He had a long stick and walked around from place to place. His stick had a hook on the end of it to help him along. He shuffled along the road."

"What was his district?"
"He went way down the back way somewhere. North Otago seemed to be his centre, and he stopped at the back of the Empire Hotel in the stables with several other swaggers, such as Willie Pinket and The Scottish Blue Boy."

"The name Barney White Rats—because he carried white Rats?"
"I have heard that, but I have never seen him with rats or know of anyone who has. It was just handed down that he used to have performing white mice. He might have had them at one stage. The tale the way I heard it was that he kept them inside his shirt, and used to feed them on breadcrumbs.

Whether that was correct or not I don't know. I don't think there is anyone alive who could prove or tell you."

Curiously, John Stevenson at 87, still remembers Barney's 'box' rather than performances 80 years ago around Dunback. In illfitting white moleskin trousers and blue denim jacket with pockets, Barney camped in a stable and carried on his back his box, some 18 inches wide, two feet long, and six inches deep. It had three moleskin-partitioned peep-holes, each three inches square and each containing a different sized mouse. A child paid a penny per peep per hole. No tricks were performed, as far as John could remember: only the colour and different sizes of the mice were the attraction—but another 87-year-old, Alan J. McKenzie, confirming this peep-hole show, says the animals ran around on swings and slides within Barney's darkened box, but did not perform.

His beat ranged from Invercargill to as far north at times as Timaru, and even apparently to the North Island in his earlier swagging days, for as one note records: "The only occasions on which he would condescend to accept a lift were when he crossed Cook Strait."

For half a century he was a regular caller at Pukeuri, exchanging yarns of the sea for a shakedown, because he and Mr Orbell had travelled together to New Zealand on the same ship.

Two other friends, in Otago, were Dinney Daley (a bullock waggoner often carting about three-ton loads of coal with six somewhat scrawny bullocks) and Yankee Bill (Bill Anthony): Barney and Bill thought nothing of walking nine miles to the pub—and running the last 100 yards!

In his old age Barney White Rats would spell up for a bit in an old men's home, gather strength, then hit the road again, and incredibly he kept on like this to within a mere three months of his death, at 90, at Oamaru's Victoria Home on 13 July, 1911. Nothing marks his pauper's grave.

Undoubtedly, unforgettably, the highlight of Barney's visit, to Jessie H. Wallace's generation at Roxburgh school 70 years ago, was when he wet on the floor.

The last word from the other small girl in his audience of

long ago, Mrs Margaret White of Dunedin, who went to school and lived at Waikouaiti from the 1880s to 1930, writing now at 93 and blind, through her friend Mrs Tui Fox:

"One of my pleasant memories of Barney is of him and his two white mice. He would have the mice in a box which he swagged on his back while walking from school to school. Mr Moore, our schoolmaster, looked forward to his visits and was very kind to him. He used to give him boots, but Barney used to sell these at the pub.

"He used to charge twopence to see his mice, but one day I never had the money to see them, so I started on my four-mile walk home to Shag Valley. Meeting Barney going towards the school, I stopped him and asked:

" 'Could I see your mice, please?'

" 'Why aren't you at school?' answered Barney.

"I said I never had the twopence, so he put his hand in his pocket, gave me the money, and told me to go back to school and watch the show."

A night out lying against Otago's large red tussocks or manuka—that was nothing to Jack Frale—he never bothered to carry even a small tent. A most likeable old man with a medium beard and always a black felt hat, his swag-sack had one strap only, slung over one shoulder, Jim Roberts remembers, and a stick across his back hooked in his two elbows. His beat at the beginning of this century was between Mossburn and Te Anau, taking 18 months to two years. He was a slow walker, and a good many hotels lay scattered around the countryside then. Jack had several teeth left, but wrapped a large hunk of string round his pipe stem, to clamp it in his gums.

An associate, much younger, known to the whole district as Soldier Bill (Bill Page) had served on India's North West Frontier, but now went rabbiting. He always wore a bowler hat, leggings and riding britches with a saucer-shaped kneepad for kneeling when setting traps. Soldier Bill left New Zealand with the Main Body and was killed at Gallipoli.

A parade now of Southland swaggers around the turn of the century, from a singer to a Chinese. One who arrived at a Mataura home the worse for drink, sat up behind the table and insisted on singing for his supper. The song was all about 'Sweet Alice Ben Boult', and Alice trembling with fear at his frown. This swagger's name is not known—but it could well have been Tommy Tucker.

'Insicks' was so nicknamed because he refused to sleep in the barn, saying he was scared of rats and 'insicks'. Instead, he slept in the dray which was kept in an open-fronted cart shed, much less comfortable than the barn would have been.

Paddy Troye, watching grandfather toasting his unusually small feet before the fire, gave the patriarch's bare foot a slap this way and that and remarked: "Did you ever see such a fut on a pig or a dog?"

Another chuckled over French novels, and a scholar-swagman quoted Milton to a woman bathing in a creek in an orchard at Alexandra: *Sabrina fair, listen where thou art sitting, Under the glassie, cool translucent wave.*

One, (named Lamond?) always carried books in his swag, and never failed to call on the late Finlay MacKay of Reay for a discussion on intellectual matters. Others again were not exactly desirable guests at the table, such as one who after finishing his porridge, emptied the remains of his milk back into the jug. Another Southland traveller insisted on always taking bread from the table to feed his dog; and a Chinese, who arrived at the door asking, "Piece-a-billy?" (food) was deeply offended when grandmother offered him some rice pudding left over from dinner that day.

During a long country life, Prue M. Henderson, 84, now of Christchurch, says the most polite and gentlemanly swagger of the lot was a Chinese, who asked only for a drink of tea, but when given milk and food as well was so grateful, "and left saying I'd never go hungry, for helping a hungry man along life's way."

Many swaggers were given meals as the quickest and easiest way of getting rid of them, but one traveller is reputed to have carried a handful of horse manure, which he produced on receiving a grim reception, remarking he was so hungry he'd have to eat that.

This worked well, until he approached a dour old pinchpenny Scot, who shook his head until the manure was exhibited. At this, he brightened considerably.

"Hoots mon, dinna eat that!" he exclaimed jovially. "Come doon the stable, and I'll gee-ye some fresh stuff."

Humorous and very honest, The Spinner, wellknown for his stories, travelled the coastal route. Floods forced him to take a remote road further inland, seldom if ever used by swaggers, and the startled and tense woman at the farmhouse door, answering his knock, handed him a billy of very weak tea and a lump of dry bread, saying:

"It is not for my sake and not for your sake, but for the Lord Jesus sake that I give you this food."

The Spinner looked at the bread, and then at her, and answered:

"Lady, not for my sake and not for your sake, but for the Lord Jesus sake put a bit of butter on it."

He got his request, thanked her, bowed gracefully, and went on his way.

After an interminable saying of grace, one traveller had to satisfy his hunger with sharing water biscuits and a jug of water, remembers John McCaw, and remarking later: "I wonder just how long the old devil would have gone on if there'd *really* been something to be thankful for?"

Returning once more to 92-year-old Gilbert Nisbet's tape recording:

"What about women swaggers?"

"Yes I have seen two on the road, with men, old Bridget Dicks was one and the police came out in a four-wheeled express and took her in. It took four policemen to take her."

"Then a woman swagger called Mary the Man?"

"I met and knew her. She was a big tall woman, McWinnie was her name, and she lived up in the old barracks on the cape (Wanbrow) in the immigrant barracks. Her mother was carried from a boat way out at sea and the Maoris carried her in on their backs."

"There were swaggers then and also men on the swag who were not professional swaggers, moving from job to job."
"Quite a few of them never worked. They just went to doors for handouts and onto the next place."

"On the turn-in about 12 miles south of Oamaru and 3 miles inland, you turn into Gemmels Crossing, and there is an old building nearly fallen down—was this once 'The Swaggers' rest'?"
"That was at Otira Station just when you cross the bridge at Wairek. It was the old Otira cookhouse where the men who worked on the station lived. The swaggers, after the station broke up, used to settle there for the night in the old kitchen with an open fire."

"Wasn't one of these swaggers quite an artist?"
"Yes. I saw that art. All the walls were whitewashed and on one wall was a charcoal sketch of Dick Seddon, in full life size, the living image of him! The swagger who drew it must have been a real artist. Booze got the better of him probably, that's why he turned swagger."

"The last swagger I recall in this district had a round of the North Otago District."
"Yes. He was always talking to himself about property—I don't know his name. The last time he came to our place was a wet stormy day and he came to the door to get something to eat. Mum made him sit down in the wash house and she gave him a plate of soup and then she took out some meat and bread and that was the last we saw of him—he was killed in the street a night or two after."

"You knew The Shiner?"
"When I was a kid about four years old I can remember him. He was a notorious hard-shot swagger. I used to see him all over the country, especially at Mickie Doyle's pub at Weston."

"There were other ones as well—The Bear."
"Billy the Bear—I worked with him up at Haka Station. He

actually worked as well as swagging, shearing the sheep. He would arrive with a pair of nice clean moleskins on and we would be six weeks shearing and you should have seen them—they would stand up on their own."

"A certain swagger who came into a title in England?"
"That was Ayers. His wife lived in Oamaru and he was fencing up at Elderslie. One of the Earls, (the Earl of Seafield or the Lord Redheavan, I am not sure which, Earl of Seafield I think) died and he was next in line to the title. But as soon as he got word he rolled up his blankets and was coming towards Oamaru. He was a swagger when he was not working.

"Now Neil Fleming was one of the leading lights here in Oamaru. Fleming and Headley—they had the big stables down here. When he heard it he hooked up a flash buggy and a pair of nice black shining horses to meet the Earl.

"He met him all right.

" 'Come in, my Earl,' he says.

"The Earl of Seafield looked at him and said:

" 'Look boy, you have passed me many times, and you can pass me again.'

"He died here in Oamaru and his grave is up in the far top corner of the cemetery. I think he was buried under the title of Lord Redheavan."

Moving north again, an ancient swagger with the engaging name of Henry Moon drifted back and forth through the Mackenzie Country, and another veteran, wearily passing through Fairlie, sat down under a pine tree to rest, and was found there a week later—the end of the road.

Another hardcase rover, Archie McVee, told Jim Capill how once in a snowstorm coming back to his hut, he knew he was in the right place, but blowed if he could find the hut anywhere. He kept on searching until suddenly the snow gave way, and he fell down the chimney!

Another time out on a road a wild pig charged him, a great savage boar. All he had to protect himself with was a large piece of willow stick, and this he hurled at the mad

'She Could Have Nearly Howled'

Captain Cooker. It stuck in his back, around about his kidneys. Archie thought he'd killed him, and left him there. About a year later, returning on his beat, on the same road he sat down beside a young willow tree and thought vaguely: "That wasn't here last time?" All of a sudden the willow tree started to move—and there was the porker, ambling off with the willow tree that had taken root!

A cunning old coot criss-crossing the Mackenzie Country cooked occasionally on Clayton Station. He would go sporadically into Fairlie on the spree, sometimes taking with him a four-gallon tin of fat which they let him save to hock off for beer.

At Clayton they had been missing stores from time to time, and couldn't nab the culprit, until someone got the bright idea of digging into one of the tins of fat. There, under about an inch of fat, were sultanas, raisins, and so forth, neatly 'acquired' from the stores!

Some thief had stolen the grindstone from Orari Station, Basil Borthwick will tell you. The system at Orari Station was that swaggers would report to Charlie Tripp, knowing that he was always well disposed to a man who could produce a pocketful of dead wool or wool collected off a barbed wire fence. Some stations ran a ticket system, but there were no tickets at Orari and Mr Tripp would say, "Down to the hut, spuds and mutton." At the hut they were issued with a ration to cook themselves.

Naturally, the word about the grindstone soon got about, and the swaggers, when handing over a pocketful of wool, learned the trick of saying:

"By the way, Mr Tripp, I saw a grindstone."

His response was immediate. Before they had finished saying the word 'grindstone', Mr Tripp would raise his right hand and shout: "That's mine."

Dozing away on a train trip, Tripp was partly awakened by the guard asking: "Ticket please." To the guard's mystification, Tripp replied: "No ticket. Spuds and meat at the cookhouse."

Several Mackenzie Country housewives were mildly startled when The Dog Swagger, in dark suit with large looping watch chain, poured milk into his billy lid, smilingly watched his small pet terrier-type dog lap away, then lifted the lid to finish the remainder himself.

Dogged and determined, Pegleg, wellknown about Geraldine, was a one-legged travelling tinsmith who certainly got around. With his soldering iron and gear, he'd fix anything on the spot, a cheerful man, unfortunately an early fatal victim of the motorcar, bowled over on the main road between Geraldine and Winchester.

A different fate awaited an Irishman, who H. J. Kavanagh of Bryndwr still holds in respect:

Jack McKnight would periodically call on my grandfather Edmund Noonan of Hornby who had arrived in New Zealand from Ireland about the same time as Jack, in the 1870s. Jack was singular in this respect: he was not an itinerant forced on the swag as so many of them were through hardship.

He took to the swag from the day he set foot in New Zealand. For half a century at least he contrived to exist on the 'hospitality' (a shakedown in a farmer's shed, supper, breakfast and an early departure) of the next cockie on the next stage of his journey to anywhere in the South Island.

He had memorised long passages from Darwin and Huxley, and it was the recitation of these, which of course I was too young to understand, which makes the deepest impression on my memory.

Jack was finally forced off the road in the saddest circumstances. He turned up at my grandfather's place one day about 1928 complaining of trouble which had developed in one of his ears. He was taken to hospital where examination revealed an advanced stage of cancer.

Avoiding the highways, a teetotaller, loving rationalistic literature, smoking his old clay pipe, and discoursing, always at the top of his voice, with friends of his own choosing . . . I cherish my memory of Jack McKnight for the joviality which never failed him. He was a 'natural' for the road.

And to sum up Jack McKnight, Mr Kavanagh adds:

"It is my firm conviction that he was about the most remarkable character who ever walked the roads of this country. Besides his remarkable memory, he was a philosopher in his own right. He had the bible by heart as well as Darwin, and could confute orthodox believers on their own ground. Strangely enough his long solitary rambles never destroyed his openness when in company.

"He might be described as a sort of secular saint. His opinions he proclaimed in his Irish manner, forthrightly, for you to take them or leave them.

" 'Mrs Noonan,' he would say to my grandmother, a staunch Roman Catholic, 'when you die the world dies with you.'

"My aunt, now 86, tells me that as children they delighted in his coming. He would lilt ditties, accompanying himself with firetongs, presumably on the fender.

"His aversion for work was profound but he humped a swag which few labourers would carry for double the daily wage rate."

The Christchurch area seemed to be a good re-stocking depot, or launching pad, for South Island swaggers.

Holiday time at Strowan House at St Andrews College, Papanui Road, during the August holidays, and in response to loud and repeated ringing of the front door bell, Miss Westbrooke answered.

There stood a tall bearded swagger. He raised a battered bun hat.

"Good morning ma'am. Would it be possible, do you think, to let me have a few tacks? And the loan of a tack-hammer?"

He pointed to his boots: one gaped an open mouth, the toes wriggling like a tongue: "I'd be much obliged."

Miss Westbrooke goggled a bit. Swaggers were nothing new during the holidays, but usually they came through the back entrance, to the staff quarters, and did their tasks in return for a meal and a well stocked pack.

"Of course," she said. "But you'll have to go round to the back door. You should have done that in the first place."

The man drew himself up. "That I won't."

The bun hat was jammed back on the shaggy head.

"I'm none of your tramps, ma'am. *I'm a gentleman of the road.*"

Never was a man refused a shakedown and meal at Glentui, a wellknown camping place during the hungry 1930s when swaggers were many, writes Allan Macdonald of Rangiora, who affectionately recalls three visitors:

'Quebec', on foot with the usual swag and black billy, turned down for a bed for the night and a feed at Gorge Camp, and telling me wrathfully: "Here am I paying rates and taxes to keep those . . . .s in a job and they hunted me on!"

Offered tucker and shelter, Quebec said "Thanks, Mac," and pressed on, still muttering his opinion of teamsters.

An unusual pair, seemingly without a care in the world, camped many a time at Glentui: Mathew Russel, short, nuggety, bushy beard and rather long hair, clad in an old frock coat down below the knees, with a battered bowler hat. Ned Farquharson, tall, thin, bushy moustache, wearing a pair of ladies' riding pants a size too small.

One day a sudden storm came up, I galloped to the nearest shelter, the old Jennings Camp, dropped the reins and rushed inside. A huge fire roared up the chimney. In the middle of the floor a large heap of straw. To my astonishment the bushy, bearded head of Mathew Russel appeared from the centre of the heap.

"Mathew! You'll set the place on fire, and you with it!"

"Don't worry Mac," was his reply, "I knows me straw."

Ned Farquharson I met one morning at the Black Hut. "Hullo Ned, what do you think of the weather?" Looking at the sky in all directions and deliberating for a full minute he replied: "It might rain and it might not."

'Comrade Shellback' claimed to have been a sailor, says K. Harrison of Christchurch. He had definite Left political views, invariably addressing everyone as 'Comrade'.

His usual beat was north from Christchurch to the Cheviot-Kaikoura area, and his visits were usually three to four months apart.

He was never known to have done any work.

'Scotty' (Alex) Martin, a Scot, came out to New Zealand

'She Could Have Nearly Howled'

as a young man, a remittance man, I think, as he always made for Kaikoura, remembers John B. Buchanan of Mataura. I heard he died between Waiau and Kaikoura. He used to call at the Lyndon and Mount Paul Stations, owned by the brothers Jim and Charles McFarlane.

He was always very tidy and wore a cap. He had his rounds and always arrived at night, carried a light swag, and had a trim short beard.

How many today beside the storied Awatere River remember when Scotty Martin passed through Upton Fells in a hurry in April 1929, telling Eric Baynon the shepherd he was hotfooting it to Blenheim at all costs. Sorry he couldn't linger, he was on a time limit to get to Blenheim to see Harry Lauder, the Scots comedian.

"And what did you think of Harry Lauder?" Eric asked him, on his next trip.

Scotty nearly bust himself laughing, and described how he got to Blenheim all right, arriving one day too soon, "So you see, I filled in the time celebrating, ha ha!"

During celebrations he met Constable Tim Healey, and Tim was The Law in those days, a big fellow with a fatherly interest in all—he had to supply Scotty with Government accommodation.

"So," laughed Scotty, "I didn't hear Harry Lauder after all!"

And Janice Little of Rangiora adds:

Scotty Martin was quite wellknown in North Canterbury on the stations. He arrived at Mount Vulcan one shearing time and my mother-in-law told him he could have a bunk in the shearers' quarters (about 12 men and a cook in residence just then), but he preferred to sleep on some hay in the stable "because," as he said, "you can't trust them, they're a wandering mob, here today and gone tomorrow."

What's more, he wouldn't have a meal with them either, taking his breakfast with us at the house!

Scotty's rounds were generally reasonably up to time, and if he didn't turn up at the next place inquiries would be likely, asking where was his last call and where was he heading? Over the phone in leisurely wide-ranging chat, the 'girls' would discuss his whereabouts:

"Oh, he's not here yet, but at so-and-so's."

Knowing Scotty's age—he was in his 60s—and health, they'd say:

"Um . . . Better find out where he is if there's no sign."

Usually more travelling was done in summertime, and in the heat Scotty probably got tired and went under this bridge for keeps, his heart maybe wearying for a rest. It's possible Scotty "ran out of time" (to use Ann Bradley's apt expression) in the Waipara area, about 30 miles from Christchurch, the year about 1932, a friend estimates.

A fellow-countryman—the two may have been confused here and there perhaps—was 'Scotty' Fraser, who could plunge into politics while the porridge grew cold untasted, the chops smoked unheeded in the pan and the children listened openmouthed.

He knew the inland route from Waiau to Kaikoura very well, some saying on reaching Kaikoura he'd go south as far as Waipara, then up through Waikari, Hawarden, Culverden, Hanmer and back to Waiau.

"Poor old Scotty. He died a lonely death, on his own, in the great outdoors, and who knows, perhaps this was the way he wanted it to be," sums up Basil Borthwick of Christchurch. "Nobody knew and nobody missed him.

"Now the original Charwell Forks School had a sunny porch, and I think many a swagger would shelter there in bad weather.

"Scotty's remains were found among the tussocks not far from the road in the Charwell Forks district, and were collected by Constable McLennan, who was at the Kaikoura police station from 1926 to 1941."

Cashing in on his undoubted charm to win good meals and comfy beds, the Gentleman Swagger (Broomhall-Smith) had been an officer in the Navy, "presentable in every way . . . and more than likely he would remain for a week," wrote E. C. Studholme in *Te Waimate*.

A Norwegian sailor in the closing years of last century spent part of the year at sea, the rest ashore, swaggering round South Island farms to repair horse and cow covers, good at canvas work, and saying he felt convinced New Zealand would never carry a big population because we had too much broken country and were too far from the world markets.

Said to have been first officer on a Spanish man-o'-war, 'The King of Swaggers' (also called Jimmy Wilson, but his real name was never known) deserted for the goldrush in Gabriels Gully, reputedly spoke five languages, and was keen on mathematics, history, and astronomy. A. C. Mathieson of Longwood, Riverton, writes how his father, farming at Benmore 65 to 70 years ago, remembered 'The King of Swaggers' then in his old age, his area Waimea Plains from Lumsden down to Awarua Plains: "a well-built man with a very prominent forehead, well respected wherever he went, spoke with a deep bass voice, very tidy and clean, and carried a very heavy swag containing many trinkets which belonged to him when serving in the Navy. He was, he said, 84 years old when he was challenged by a student at figures—and he beat the student outright."

Probably the first swaggers were runaway sailors—they wanted to put as much distance as possible between themselves and the ship, so they struck out for the back-country stations. A group of sailors jumped ship at Lyttelton, and the most distant place they could think of was Greymouth. After a gruelling fortnight they arrived—thankfully dropped into a handy pub and behold! there was the captain and first mate. They bolted smartly without being seen—the ship had sailed round the coast in about the same time as they had been struggling overland!

"Ahead, on a hot, dusty road, a shabby old man limped," Roey Winn of Fendalton writes for our collection, "and as we drew level, he looked at us pleadingly, so my husband broke his rule against picking up strangers and stopped the car to offer a lift. The limp disappeared.

" 'Half a mo, mister, I'll get me pack.'

"From behind a clump of broom on the roadside he dragged a filthy bedroll with a fryingpan and a billy dangling from it. I wondered how many times he'd limped a few paces each time a car approached.

"My husband's face was a map of dismay when the pack was flung onto the cream leather seat and the door shut with a crash.

"We were staying at a wayside hotel at Hurunui, and had spent the day scrambling about the hills.

"By a bridge not far from the pub, the swagger asked if we'd let him down. He was given ten shillings and told to buy a few beers when he needed them.

"'Never touch the stuff,' the old man said. 'But I need food real bad. I've got a couple of eggs for me tea, and I'll bed down under the bridge for the night.'

"Compassionate, and a bit ashamed of the ten shillings, my husband handed over a pound, real money in the early 1940s, and suggested that the old chap should buy chops and bread at the next store he came upon, and reminded him there was a pub close by.

"He seemed anxious to get rid of us, so we drove round the bend to the hotel, parked the car in a shed at the back, and washed off the dust of our hill scramblings. Half an hour later my husband went to the door of the bar, and there was our swagger, several beers to the good, talking hard about the long, weary tramp he'd had since early morning, how he'd chopped wood at a farm to get the miserly ten shillings for the beer he needed to make up for lost sweat, and how he didn't have a penny for food.

"The kindly man behind the bar told him he could get a feed in the kitchen.

"'First bit of kindness I've had in weeks,' he said humbly. The barman put his halo straight.

"Swaggie turned round and saw my husband who, to avoid embarrassing the old humbug, went outside again, and stood where he could hear. He heard enough to prove the adage that listeners hear no good of themselves.

"'Y'h saw that bloke? Arr—no wonder he wouldn't face me. The bastard only laughed and didn't stop to give me a lift when he muster seen I could 'ardly walk.'

"My husband, who had a kinky sense of humour, didn't

defend himself, but decided that he'd never again pick up another swagger, with or without a limp."

John A. Lee takes over to tell of a musical swagger:

Piccolo Charlie and his dog wandered the roads of Canterbury and visited the mining areas on the West Coast in the heyday of gold getting.

He wintered in the Hokitika jail where he lived in a cell that was never locked. The constable and his wife accommodated Charlie and his dog, and Charlie chopped enough wood to last until the next winter, dug the garden, did odd jobs and played his piccolo to the constable, his wife and dog.

When spring came, he rolled his swag, called his dog, bade the constable goodbye and walked over the mountains to Canterbury, stopping to play his piccolo and putting his hat down to receive the reward of those who appreciated good music.

He would move around in Canterbury, cross back and do the mining camps on the West Coast. In one town of the West Coast he took his dog, himself and piccolo down to where the Greymouth breakwater was being made. A big group of observers were standing round the piledriver.

"What's up?" Piccolo Charlie asked.

"The monkey is drowned. It's fallen off into the river."

Piccolo Charlie put down his hat, put his piccolo to his lips and played the Dead March for the drowned monkey. The coins showered into his hat.

Ah—but music can be sweet or sour to the ear . . .

Wan and tired after his long trudge along gravel roads and through unbridged streams in South Westland, poor Bill with his swag reached the farm, was not afraid of work, but his one defect, whistling incessantly the one dolorous tune *The Letter Edged in Black,* infuriated Ivy Crozier's father.

Patience wearing thin after several weeks of this dismal tune, dad exclaimed:

"Either stop this confounded whistle or go!"

Detesting the hard roads, poor Bill did his best, couldn't stop however, became utterly miserable and reluctantly shouldered his pack, again.

"We could only hope he found some place else where his *Letter Edged in Black* was appreciated," writes Ivy.

"I would like to say a good word for the swagger," writes C. S. Vigers of Dannevirke. "In my association with hundreds of them, I never knew one to be dishonest or interfere with property."

With a roll-call all of his own, he produces six swaggers and a cricketer who roamed the highways and byways of the East Coast some 50 years ago, regularly calling on stations there:

The Timaru Pirate: I remember him calling on the cook to report his arrival a little earlier than usual. The cook, a Cockney, greeted him with: "Wot, you 'ere again?" And Pirate replied: "Yes, and if it is any b .... news to you I'll be 'ere again."

Bluey or Wingie: He only had one arm, was a 'meth king'; his colour used to turn to a vivid blue when on the meths; even with his one arm he was quite a good scrubcutter.

Lousy Cockney: The station hands on a certain station would give him a bath with Little's dip in it sometimes; the boss would give him one of his old suits and a pair of boots.

Psyche: Got his name after a shepherd saw him bathing his feet in a pool on the side of the road. 'Psyche at the Well' was a bit of a character and quite humorous.

Russian Jack: A powerfully-built man, he told me that his first job in New Zealand was cutting scrub but he was never paid for it, so swore he would never work again.

The Shrewd Pea: used to talk to himself when on the move, but when accused of this said he was in communication with the Banshees, 'Irish female fairies'. This chap knew all the happenings on every station from Waiorongomai to Mangaohane. He used to leave the coast occasionally and go inland over Gentle Annie to the back of Taihape.

There were many more in those days, but they were not so colourful.

Men from all walks of life roamed the countryside during the '30s depression—clerks, mechanics, carpenters, etc.

'She Could Have Nearly Howled' 195

The boss on the station where I worked was a keen cricketer, and could put a full team on the field. We were having a practice when a swagman pulled up, sat on his swag, and watched.

The boss went over to him and asked: "Do you know anything about this game?" He said he'd played one time, so the boss went off, got him a pair of boots, and he took his place in the field.

As soon as he walked on, I could see that he had a fair knowledge of what was what.

When it came his turn to bat we could not get the old beggar out. The boss gave him a job helping the cook for the rest of the cricket season, and also supplied him with gear. We found out later he had represented his Province many years before.

On some occasions it wasn't done to ask a swagman his original occupation. Don McLennan of Palmerston North says three gave him the answer he deserved when he asked:

"What did you do for a crust?"

One said he was a 'sniffer' in a brewery, sniffing the empty bottles before they were refilled to detect any bottles with dregs of kerosene, disinfectant, turps, etc. "A good job," said Tom, "when you got a cold you got a day orf."

Another chap replied that he was a fretworker: "I work one day and fret the rest of the week."

The other bloke, who said his name was Mick Hooper, explained that he was a second carpenter . . . he built the little houses behind the big ones.

The longer one North Island swagger stayed unemployed, the better. He was Tom Long the Hangman, who made regular circuits through the Wairarapa around the 1900s. Apparently Tom was the government hangman and received five pounds for each hanging. When not in work he roamed the country as a swagger.

Tim Donovan, a wellknown scrubcutting contractor out the back of Martinborough, had a good deal of experience with swagmen, and W. Andrew of Te Puke tells how Tim employed about 20 men—three gangs, one coming, one working, one going! If anyone went to him for a job, Tim would ask:

"Have you done time?"

"Yes."

"The job is yours."

One day Tim told his cook:

"I've got a full gang again. They have all done time."

Then on a quick visit to Martinborough he heard a whisper that the policeman was on his way out to the camp to pick up somebody.

"Tim headed back fast to give the chap warning, arriving just when the boys were in the galley having tea, and announced:

" 'The policeman is on his way out to collect one of you lads. You'll know which one of you it is.'

"That night, all hands slept in the bush."

These old boys of the road had a wonderful sense of smell (W. Andrew, a countryman born in 1892, continues), and could nose out a bottle of grog a mile away. A mate went for a trip in his car to the Wairarapa and ran out of petrol in a remote spot. Luckily, he had a bottle of whisky under the seat. In desperation he put that into the tank, with wonderful results—the old bomb seemed to be enjoying it.

He also noticed every time he passed a swaggie on the road the swaggie would drop his swag *and come racing up behind with his nose in the air* . . .

A familiar sight around the Wanganui district roadside in 1908-12 was white bundles under the bushes and fences, sometimes solitary, sometimes two or three together. A stranger passing by early could be perplexed, until he noticed these were swaggers, curled up under a gorse fence or by some natural shelter, covered with newspapers to keep the blankets dry from the dew.

The man whose heart, mind and soul were in the countryside, Archdeacon James Young, of Westland, Wellington and Nelson provinces, enjoyed telling of a young auctioneer travelling to conduct his first stock sale, and feeling a little uncertain, stopped in the middle of a long stretch of road in the King Country, got out of his car, mounted a stump, and began a spirited auction:

"Now here we have, gentlemen, a pen of fine young steers. Somebody start me with a bid per head. Anyone say $-.-? $-.- then. Come on, give me a start of $-.- then . . . $-.-, $-.- I'm bid $-.-, what advance on $-.-."

With that, an elderly swagger, roused from his sleep from under a nearby bush, roared:

"Knock 'em down you fool; they're not worth half the money!"

The young auctioneer bolted, the story spread, and for years his auctions would be interrupted with a shout from the back, or a whisper from beside him:

"Knock 'em down you fool—they're not worth half the money!"

The mother of the owner of Akitio Station, Dannevirke way, had a soft spot for swaggers. Evidently one had done her a good turn some time ago, and she asked her son to build a special whare for them. He did: a six-bunk place with mattresses. Said one of the station hands: "We always knew when she was paying a visit to the station, because the boss would send the cowboy up to clean the place out and put in a stock of firewood. The first thing she'd do on arrival was to inspect the swagger whare!"

A veteran in the Gisborne district was on the road with a mob of sheep when he was caught up by a swagman, asking:

"Mister, got a spare cigarette?"

"I'm sorry mate," he said, "but I smoked my last cigarette after breakfast and I won't be able to get any more until I get to the store ten miles away."

"Oh, that's no good. You can't go all that long without a smoke," sympathised the swagman, and pulled out of his pocket a canvas bag, which was full of small ends of plug tobacco, home made cigarettes, and loose tobacco. "Here," he said. "Help yourself!"

"Good day, Mr Swagman," said John Gale, salesman for Shell oil, returning on the Skippers road to Queentown.

"Swagman, Esquire!" came the reply with a grin.

They shared John's lunchbox and thermos tea, and he turned out to be a remittance man thoroughly enjoying life as a swagger.

"This is good tea," he said. "But I enjoy lemon tea. Yes. They always used to cut a slice of lemon for me."

John offered the swagger a cigarette. He politely asked for two or three, pulling out a short-stem clay pipe and stuffing three cigarettes into the well-charred bowl.

One swagger is said to have had a special pipe without a bottom to its bowl. When offered tobacco, with dexterous and concealing use of his right hand, this man could stuff an enormous amount into his pipe, and did.

Stan Knowles of Tauranga remembers how at Hatuma, Hawkes Bay, 1924, a group of swaggers one evening set up camp in a plantation alongside the school.

Claiming that the campers were "frightening the womenfolk," somebody did a hurried trip around the scattered community to organise a 'turn-them-out' squad.

As the swaggers settled comfortably (and harmlessly) about their campfire, a strong body of men descended upon them, and forced them to strike camp and move on.

Even individual reactions were sometimes not particularly friendly as this little New Zealand homespun verse of the time (author unknown) indicates:

> *The swagger is a lonely man,*
> *And sometimes very old,*
> *And every day he wanders round,*
> *Like a lost sheep from the fold,*
> *It's baccy here, hot water there,*
> *Perhaps a drop of tea,*
> *But if you say 'Go chop some wood,'*
> *Then down the road he'll flee.*

Grateful to get in out of the wind and cold, this almost worn-out walker of the endless road, after tea asked for a piece of cotton, produced from his pocket a good fistful of threepences with holes punched in them, and with hands so shaky he could scarcely push the cotton through the holes,

'She Could Have Nearly Howled' 199

threaded the lot together. He next courteously gave threepence to each child in this Southern Hawkes Bay family, and sixpence to the baby.

He with nothing gave love.

Old John came off the roads to stay at Effie Best's backcountry farm on the Papamoa Hills, do odd jobs, build the fires, watch over the children and tell them of his shipboard days and adventures. Occasionally he'd get thirsty, disappear for a few days, then return very repentant with a big bag of bananas.

Once when Mr Best was reading about the Macquarie Islands he jumped up from the table, upsetting his chair, crying: "Good God! That's where I nearly left my bloody bones!"

He explained he was to have gone on a boat to rescue people stranded on the island—but he'd feigned apoplexy by eating soap. The crew had to sail without him. The boat was lost with all hands aboard.

Mr Best's father, William, was captain of this doomed ship, the *Kakanui!* Nineteen men went down with this unseaworthy ship when enveloped in a storm at the end of 1890.

I listened in fascination to the story of Jack Logan, this tiny white-bearded man who, over seventy years ago, arrived every year to spend the winter in a shed on a property at Whetukura near Ormondville (writes Kathleen Yule from Hastings).

Each year the children waited expectantly for his arrival. Here he was, as usual, his roll of swag on his back and his shiny little billy gleaming. A diminutive dog named Lucy, as white as old Jack's whiskers, was always his companion. Dear old Jack—his beard and everything about him as clean as could be—famous for his beautiful camp-oven bread that brought the family to visit him as soon as the first appetising whiff reached them.

Why did his pants always sag in that untidy way? Anyone got a spare pair of braces? For years the family would say, "Hitch up your trousers, you're a real Jack Logan." But it was affectionate fun they made of him. Jack Logan came and went, and always a welcome waited for him when he arrived out of the blue to winter at Whetukura.

Back to a Canterbury echo, to Herbert Sewell speaking:

"You'd see some funny things in these old swags, you know.

"I remember taking breakfast to one old chap on his own. I think he was a Dane, and he'd had all his worldly goods out there and was wrapping them up, and he'd a set of baby's clothes. Yeah.

"I dunno—I thought about it . . .

"I told one old woman about it—she said she could have nearly howled."

From the Author to his Readers

QUICKLY seek and send any stories, memories, names, feelings, incidents, routes, photographs of swaggers you may have, or could get from veterans, no matter how slim, to the author:

Jim Henderson,
c/- Hodder & Stoughton Ltd.,
PO Box 39038, Auckland West

and we will have a second book on swaggers—but hurry, because links which can never be replaced are vanishing every day. Thank you.
"If only I'd known!" is the customary and rather craven excuse for dodging the very real toil of actually thinking out words and writing them down.
Well, now's your chance—and we certainly could add odd characters to our 'Dags' chapter too, such a change from the Grey Ones who seem to breed and multiply so alarmingly.
This book would have been impossible without the *NZ Farmer* magazine, publishing each fortnight our 'Home Country' feature. Here, among all sorts of subjects and experiences, we began collecting swaggers five years ago, and making valued contacts. To the *Farmer,* and its wide mesh of reader-contributors throughout New Zealand, my special thanks, particularly to Ray Kirk and Noel Vautier, so generously hunting for me, and to Joy Shepard. Among old 'Open Country' radio friends playing their part, thank you Violet Kerr, Elva J. Sonntag, Doreen Ann Goss, and Radio Masterton. *HMS Lion* carnage is from *Jutland* by Stuart Legg.

—J.H.

Russian Jack   Comrade Shellback   Ned Sl
                                   'The Sl